The Quality Analects of
Mr. Funny Guy

BY TIM ROGERS

I have no idea what the hell an "analect" is.

ISBN 0-9672452-0-6

Printed in the United States of America by Jerry Stinnett's Fine Printing, which was, indeed, fine.

First Edition

1 2 3 4 5 6 7 8 9 10

For the two hot babes in my life,
Christine and Terri

Props
by Tim Rogers

MANY PEOPLE DIED TO BRING YOU THE WORDS CONTAINED IN THESE pages. I owe those people, if not a portion of the proceeds, then at least a few kind words. In the vernacular of today's youth, I must render unto them their props. So then:

Much props to Eric "Does My Butt Look Big in These Dockers?" Celeste. When *The Met* began publishing, way back in April 1994, before the Internet changed everything, Eric signed me up as a columnist. He gave me the opportunity because I drank a lot and committed dangerous and/or stupid acts when I did. Eric figured stories about all that would make for great reading. His staff, notably his managing editor, Joseph Guinto, didn't cotton to the idea of my writing a weekly column about how much I drank. But Eric was a visionary. He understood that the citizens of Dallas craved stories about me and my life and my drinking. The "best" of those stories constitute the meat of this volume. Sadly, Eric was killed while attempting to smooth out a particularly jarring transition in a column I had written about a bad hangover.

Much props to Joseph "I Have No Connections to the Mafia" Guinto. When Eric met his untimely demise, Joe took the helm at *The Met* and sailed the ship into waters that had been charted, yes, but those charts were far too expensive for *The Met* to afford. Joe was a swell editor. He didn't have what you'd call a stranglehold on the rules of punctuation or grammar (the distinction between "its" and "it's" eluded him for years), but he nonetheless encouraged me not to suck. Joe perished when a dangling modifier fell on him. He never saw it coming.

Props, too, to *The Met*'s current editor, Sally "Don't Tell My Mother" Rodgers. Sally fills out the payroll forms and makes sure I get paid to write my column. We yelled at each other only hours prior to this writing, so I can't think of too many nice things to say about Sally. She has pretty eyes. These eyes will grow glassy and gray when she dies, soon.

Props to Randy "I'm Studying to Be a Spiral Wizard" Stagen, *The Met*'s publisher. Without Randy, there would be no *Met*, and, consequently, no Mr. Funny Guy. Randy recently changed his name to Rand and began conducting fire walks. He's sure to die before long.

Finally, a heaping helping of steaming props to Nick and Dawn Rizos, who own The Lodge. The first time I met them — as a guest at a Lodge-sponsored bass tournament some years back — Nick scared me. He's a swarthy man and carries a certain avoirdupois that puts less substantial fishermen ill at ease. Then there's the thick Greek accent. Nick — at the time, I was careful to call him Mr. Rizos — sounded as if he had a mouthful of sunflower seeds and was working on getting their shells off with his teeth. I had an entire conversation with Nick and understood not a single word, which was scary.

Then there was the gorgeous wife, Dawn, of whom I sensed Nick was rightfully protective. I looked her directly in the eye and did not allow my gaze to wander. Though, to my embarrassment and probably as a result of having over-served myself on the eve of the tournament, I did tell Dawn, "Fishing is a manly pursuit, and I'd wager I will land a bit more flesh than you." Or words to that effect.

The next morning, in the sober light of day, I feared for my life. A mysterious Greek man, a topless-bar magnate no less, was going to ensure that his wife won a bass tournament. My boat would have an unfortunate "accident."

Fortunately, I was wrong on all accounts. The level of the lake had dropped noticeably by midday, so many bigmouth bass did Dawn pull from its waters. This bigmouth, his boat never in danger, managed to land but one fish, and there was some dispute as to whether it was actually a fish or just a fishlike conglomerate of weeds and sticks. As for Nick, he turned out to be one of the nicest guys you could ever meet. He's really just a big Greek teddy bear — that you would treat with the utmost respect as you asked politely if it wouldn't mind repeating what it had just said.

Without Nick and Dawn and their generous support, the seven copies of *The Quality Analects of Mr. Funny Guy* would have been printed on Big Chief tablets. Please do not think I'm a shill or a whore or that I'm compromising my principles or that I've sold out or that, for the right price, I would get on all fours and bark out an endorsement for just any old product or service when I tell you that The Lodge is the finest café chantant in the whole U.S. of A. and you'd be doing yourself a disservice if you went to your grave without first paying it a visit.

Dallas, Texas
May 11, 1999

Contents:

A BUNCH OF UNANTICIPATED ROMAN-NUMERAL
CLAMJAMFRY THAT JACKED UP THE PRINTING
COSTS MORE THAN WE WOULD HAVE LIKED

Two blank, unnumbered pages   i

Title page   iii

Copyright stuff   iv

A sweet dedication   v

Yet another blank page   vi

Props   vii

Contents   ix

Forward   x

THE QUALITY ANALECTS PROPER,
WITH ARABIC NUMERALS

**Alcohol, Tobacco, and Firearms
(and Heroin and Roofies)**   1

Bodily Functions   25

Religion   43

Sex   59

Fat People, Minorities, Cripples, and Queers   83

Adventure   101

Family Life   129

A Very Special Forward
by Joseph Capasso

I MET TIM ROGERS WHILE STUDYING AT THE CISTERCIAN PREPARATORY School for young men, in Irving, Texas. I entered Cistercian in the seventh grade and so by freshman year already had two years of Catholic school experience and a gaggle of friends. I was an insider. Tim, on the other hand, attended public school until coming to Cistercian as a freshman. Tim was an outsider.

Our meeting played out like a scene from an ABC After School Special in which the new kid on the block, outrageous in manner of dress and with a too-cool-for-school attitude, tries to fit in with the established "cool guy" clique of jocks. Tim was sporting a spiked coif, a black and magenta checkered shirt, and a skinny, silver tie covered with what appeared to be glitter. Our conversation went something like this:

Me: "So you're Tim Rogers. I'm Joe Capasso. What's goin' on?"

Tim: "Nuthin'."

Me: "You goin' to the dance tonight?"

Tim: "Yeah."

Me: "Well, see ya later."

Tim: "Yeah."

Not only did I think Tim was a snappy dresser, but I found him to be an incredible asshole. As it turned out, Tim was just putting on an act. He wanted us to think he was a tough guy, but underneath that prickly exterior was a gooey, semisweet guy whom I would come to love (and not in the meet-me-at-the-bathhouse-at-9 way).

One of our teachers at Cistercian, Fr. Roch, taught us in theology class that friendships are based on one of two things. The first is a shared vice. The other is something like mutual respect or God or something. Throughout high school, my friendship with Tim grew as we discovered the vices we shared.

I knew our friendship had been firmly established when, in our senior year, Tim and I escorted each other to the Dallas Junior Symphony Ball. Tim looked divine in his purple tuxedo shirt and plaid bow tie, while I looked dashing in black leather pants and ruffled shirt. We shared a box of Vivarin and a 12-pack of Coors Light. We sang, we danced, and we frightened or enraged just about every "normal" couple at the event. Ahh, sweet vice — the grout in our wall of love.

We eventually left for college, Tim to Indiana and Notre Dame, I to the University of Texas in Austin. But while we saw each other less frequently, our time together bore bigger fruit. During one of Tim's visits to Austin, for example, with only two days of quality vice-sharing time together, we managed the following: one crashed wedding at whose reception a very loud and lengthy opinion about masturbation was forwarded (by Tim); one tripped bridesmaid (also by Tim); one bloody nose (Tim's, made so by me); one irreparably blood-stained seersucker suit (Tim's); two acts of public nakedness; and one narrowly avoided naked-guys-vs.-UT-frat-boys street brawl. Our relationship blossomed like a well-fed amaryllis.

After college, Tim and I got an apartment together in Dallas. It was during this time that he began writing his column for *The Met* and assumed his Mr. Funny Guy persona. I became the Roommate Joe character, and much of my and Tim's personal life became fodder for his weekly essays. Weekends at the apartment resembled marriage-encounter retreats, only with lots more alcohol. I remember fondly the evening we shared a few cocktails, climbed up on the roof to urinate, and wound up passing out up there, wearing only our shoes, with the front door to the apartment wide open and the stereo turned up to 10. Nor will I forget the weekend we shared some ephedrine tablets and shaved our nether regions with electric clippers in the kitchen. Our relationship, fueled by our vices and lots of free time, matured like a fine cheese.

That was a long time ago. Since then, Tim has gotten married, we've both become fathers, and, though we still pursue our vices, we've lost a few steps over the years. Children, marriage, and life in general tend to slow a man down. No more ephedrine tablets or sleeping on the roof. Now it's Enfamil and 4 a.m. bottle feedings. We've had to let God into our lives and develop a mutual respect for each other, independent of malt liquor.

Upsetting? Not really. We'll always have the memories, some of which are included in this volume. Plus, when these kids of ours are old enough, someone's got to teach them to drink.

Dallas, Texas
May 4, 1999

---○---

Alcohol, Tobacco, and Firearms (and Heroin and Roofies)

Newport Smokers Are Alive
With Pleasure

EVERY ONCE IN A WHILE, A BARTENDER WILL OVER-SERVE ME, AND MY judgment will become a little cloudy. When that happens, I sometimes beg cigarettes off friends or even strangers. Since I don't regularly smoke, I hold cigarettes awkwardly, between my thumb and forefinger, and I take aggressively long drags that make me cough, especially if whomever I bummed the cigarettes from had anything stronger than slim menthol lights.

The mornings after the nights when I occasionally get over-served and chain-smoke borrowed cigarettes, I wake up unable to breathe through my nose without whistling. This is usually accompanied by a foul paste on my tongue that I can only cure with repeated brushing.

I bring up all this unpleasantness because tobacco-industry officials have recently announced they are doing their best to fill cigarettes with tastiness and satisfaction. They claim they are not, however, trying to make cigarettes more addictive.

They are saying this because last week the *Wall Street Journal* got its hands on some internal reports produced by the world's No. 3 cigarette maker, Brown & Williamson. The reports basically detail how the tobacco industry has been trying hard to promote breast cancer and deform babies. Okay, maybe that's not technically accurate. But the reports do reveal that the tobacco industry has been tinkering with ammonia additives for decades in an effort to boost "nicotine transfer efficiencies." In other words, they've been engineering a better buzz and, in the process, making cigarettes as addictive as possible.

Now, tobacco-industry officials say we've got this all wrong. They're not adding ammonia to cigarettes to improve nicotine intake and get smokers hooked. No sir. They're only interested in improving the smooth smokability and rich aroma of their products. A representative from Brown & Williamson explained that the company adds ammonia to its cigarettes "to increase taste and flavor, reduce irritation, and to improve body."

Tobacco companies have also claimed for years that the links between smoking and cancer have not been proved. It's just that tobacco has a tendency to be used by individuals who wind up with cancer. I'm sure it's only a coincidence that the Marlboro Man,

David McLean, died from lung cancer.

Health issues aside, though, if companies like Brown & Williamson and Philip Morris are trying to make cigarettes taste good, then, in my opinion, they've still got a lot of work to do. When I wake up after a night of getting over-served and smoking, I never say, "Mmm, those Marlboros last night sure had great taste and flavor. My throat feels distinctly less irritated. And what body!" No, I usually wake up and say something like, "Blurph." Then my nose whistles.

I doubt that most people who smoke do it because they enjoy the taste of ammonia and hot carbon monoxide; they do it because they enjoy a little buzz.

If it were true that people smoked for the taste, then why doesn't Godiva make cigarette-flavored chocolates? How come Ben & Jerry's doesn't hire villagers in Central America to smoke cigarettes all day, then ship the butts to Vermont so they can make cigarette-flavored ice cream? I'm guessing they don't do it because market research has shown that people won't eat ice cream that would make their noses whistle and possibly cause them to vomit.

Coffee, on the other hand, tastes good. Caffeine can give you a dose of happy head, much like nicotine, but the java itself happens to have a pleasant flavor. That's why people eat coffee-flavored food.

But the tobacco people, fearing restrictive legislation, continue to insist the nicotine buzz is an unintended side effect that comes from enhanced flavor. They don't want to come up with new ad campaigns using only black-and-white text, as the FDA would have them do. All current cigarette ads, as you know, rely on attractive models holding cigarettes in the great outdoors.

Marlboro smokers, who live somewhere called Marlboro Country, do a lot ranch work, busting broncs and going on cattle drives and such. Kool smokers all live in the Caribbean, where they hold hands and frolic on the beach. Benson & Hedges smokers seem to be stunt men and women, able to smoke in all manner of precarious situations, including on the wings of airborne 747s. Newport smokers wear severe smiles, and they're "alive with pleasure!"

I think the FDA will have its way, though. To comply with the new regulations, I plan to launch a new brand of cigarettes, using the world's first honest cigarette ad. My cigarettes will be called Dizzies, and the black-and-white will say:

"When you're in for a hard night of drinking, don't settle for second-hand smoke. Bum a Dizzy, and go to an early grave with a buzz on."

The Scotch and Water Rendered Us Invisible to All But the Gods

USED TO THINK CONVENTIONS WERE FOR DORKS. I WOULDN'T HAVE been caught dead drunk at one. To my way of thinking, anytime you have a bunch of folks so enthusiastic about a single product, service, or idea that they'll travel across the country and stay in a hotel just to subject themselves to hours of painful small talk and awkward business-card pas de deux, then you're dealing with an assemblage of losers.

Take petcock manufacturers, for example. The petcock industry plays a vital role in the country's economic stability. And there's no disputing that petcocks are extremely useful devices. Without them, we'd have pipes and radiators everywhere filling up with unwanted or excess water, and we'd have no way to drain them. I'm sure none of us wants to see that happen. But hanging out with a bunch of petcock conventioneers isn't exactly my idea of a humdinging good time.

At least that's what I used to think. Then, last week, I attended my first convention. It took place in Nashville and was sponsored by the Association of Alternative Newsweeklies. If the AAN gig was any indicator of what goes on at all conventions, then next time the petcock manufacturers come to town, I'm busting cheeks to the front of the line for badges.

Badges, I learned, are an integral part of conventions. Badges mark conventioneers as prestigious individuals who have possibly passed lie-detector tests to receive top-level clearance. I felt like I could go to any airport in the country, flash my badge, and walk right out onto the runway.

As a direct result of my new-found self-importance, and also, I suspect, because of an open bar, I got pants-droppingly drunk the first night of the convention. At no other time in my life have I thirsted for scotch and waters, but, apparently inspired by the badge clipped to my breast pocket, I found myself sucking them down as fast as the bartender could pour them. I ordered two at a time and went back for thirds, pausing only to load up on chips and dip at the snack table.

So there I was, standing around with a bunch of conventioneers, actually convening, making small talk with a mouthful of guacamole, and it wasn't painful. Since the other ink-fingered folks were just as thirsty as I, we all got along famously. As far as I remember. My recollections of the proceedings get a little imprecise at about the point where a colleague and I absconded with a bellhop's cart and raced it through the hotel lobby, right past — I'm not kidding — Billy "Don't Yank My Beard" Gibbons from ZZ Top.

The next morning, I woke up in my clothes and dragged myself to a 9 a.m. panel discussion titled "The Joys of Filing Unnecessary Freedom of Information Act Requests," or something to that effect, and it was there that I fully came to appreciate the utility of conventions. Conventions are like college. Sure, the stuff you learn in classes comes in handy every so often, but the real payoff, the true practicality, comes from getting drunk with a select group of prestigious individuals. In college, they wear Greek letters; at conventions, they wear badges.

Once I had that all figured out, I pretty much loafed around the rest of the day, saving my energy for the evening activities and not paying much attention in class. Except when author Roy Blount Jr. got up and told a bunch jokes about interfering with sheep.

The last night of the convention, they threw a party at a place called the Parthenon, with the theme "Ode to Dionysus," which was basically like printing on the invitations: "Start your drinking early, steal the sheets off your hotel bed, and come to the party in togas." So we did. To my surprise, the aforementioned colleague and I were the only two folks to show up in proper attire. As you might expect, we were easy to spot — in the early going, that is. The bar was once again open (good thing, seeing as how wearing only boxers and the sheet left me no place to carry money), and before you could say "dues ex machina," the scotch and water had rendered us completely invisible to all but the gods. On the dance floor, I performed a high-impact, yet dignified, jig in Athena's honor. I'm sure my place at the Elysian Fields is secure.

On Monday, back at the office, my co-workers all wanted to know how the convention went. I'm typing up a memo for them, detailing the valuable things I learned while convening in Nashville. It begins: "The convention was a huge success. Everyone at the paper was well-represented. And I've got a good sheep-shagging joke if anyone wants to hear it."

I Was a Vodka-Powered Whirling Dervish Driven to a State of Religious Ecstacy
by Eddy Grant

LIKE MOST OF THESE THINGS DO, IT STARTED WITH A DARE. IT ENDED in a novel way, though, with my nearly getting beaten up by a bunch of male strippers.

A female friend of mine who was having a birthday decided that in lieu of a present, she would enjoy seeing me take my clothes off. "I dare you," she said, "to dance on amateur night at La Bare." La Bare, in case you didn't know, is "Dallas' No. 1 Ladies' Club."

A few words here about my body, and then we'll move on: I do not have a physique suitable for dancing, much less dancing unclothed. Picture Brad Pitt. Now picture Brad Pitt without his washboard stomach and without muscles in general. Then picture him with skin so pallid that he looks like he's been living in a salt mine for several years (not engaged in actual mining activities that might threaten to tone up his biceps). Then add several unattractive moles on Brad's back, and give him a bad haircut. Got the picture? Well, I look worse.

But when my friend dared me to dance at La Bare for her birthday, I figured it would get me out of having to buy her a gift.

When last Monday's amateur night arrived, I was ready. I thought, I'm going to do this thing sober. A brave man would face those screaming women without his senses clouded by what we amateur strippers call "liquid dance lessons."

Then I changed my mind and got really drunk. By the time I took the stage, I'd downed maybe five beers and at least 11 fingers of vodka.

Two other gentlemen had also signed up for amateur night. Apparently the proper procedure called for all the contestants to be introduced at once. We would then take turns performing our routines. Management must have forgotten to inform me of this, because the moment I got onstage, I started stripping.

As luck would have it, I know someone who owns a complete nun's habit, which she had loaned me so I'd have a clever costume. The DJ yelled over the PA, "Tim, stop stripping! It's not time yet. Put your clothes back on, Mother Teresa." I'm told that I yelled back, "I've got your mother right here," or words to that effect. I have to rely on what My Fair Lady and others who were present tell me, because the liquid dance lessons fouled up most of my brain's higher functions, including memory and especially motor control.

When my official turn on the stage did come, I really couldn't strip, seeing as how I was too loaded to figure out how to put the nun's habit back on. I also wore a pair of black cotton boxers that I'd modified with scissors and a little thread so they'd tear away easily. But I'd torn those off before my turn, too. So I just got up there in my pink spangly T-back thong and flounced around in an epileptic fit.

I jumped off the stage. I climbed back up. I walked on tabletops. I did the cabbage patch and the moonwalk and even a snappy bit of soft-shoe tap. I was a vodka-powered whirling dervish driven to a state of religious ecstasy by Eddy Grant, whose CD I'd selected for my dance routine. I owned "Electric Avenue."

Until I racked myself. A warning if you're thinking about participating in amateur night at La Bare and you aren't accustomed to wearing only a T-back thong: When you go to do the worm on your stomach, take care not to dive on your John Thomas.

And then came the part where I almost got my ass kicked. While we amateurs did our thing on the main stage, professional La Bare dancers boogied on smaller, auxiliary stages. I climbed up next to one of the pros and tried to do the bump with him. I think I managed a single bump before he picked me up and threw me to the floor. One of my female friends had to apologize to him and say, no, I wasn't making fun of his profession and, no, I wasn't on speed. Then the manager came over and made me sit down.

The winning amateur was picked that night by crowd reaction. He wasn't I. My friends said I came in second, but I think they were being kind. On the bright side, I did make $26 in tips. After I subtracted the cost of the T-back, and after My Fair Lady took $10 for the trouble of driving me around and pulling me out of the hedge in front of our house when we got home, that put me in the hole only $4. All things considered, a pretty cheap birthday gift.

I Took Off My Pants So I Could More Efficiently Shake My Groove Thang

I HAVE NO IDEA HOW THESE THINGS HAPPEN. EACH TIME THEY DO, I'M genuinely bewildered. There I'll be, just standing around in a bar, trying to fit in and make new friends, when a large man outfitted with a walkie-talkie and one of those flashlights that uses about eight size-D batteries will invite me to leave. Out of the blue.

There always follows a brief but intense period of silence during which everyone within a 15-foot radius of me stops what he's doing to watch the scene unfold. I stand there with my best "What? Me? What am I doing wrong?" face, while I size up the odds of making a trip to Lew Sterrett if I sucker-punch the fatboy with the flashlight and tear the place up with a pool cue for his suggesting that I was conducting myself indecorously. For his part, the bouncer inflates himself like a puffer fish at a beauty contest and adopts a expression that says, "Don't make me shine this light in your eyes."

So I begrudgingly leave and wonder why I don't get better treatment when I have to return to the bar the next day because I forgot to close my tab.

I received perhaps my most unjustified invitation to leave at a private party, for eating carrots. I had only a remote connection to the actual host, one of those friend-of-a-friend-of-somebody-who-heard-party-sounds-coming-from-that-direction relationships. But I figured that was enough. We're all brothers and sisters in God's eyes.

Well, at some point in the party, I got hungry. Since my host must have overlooked the providing-the-snacks part of his role, I jostled my way through a crowded kitchen to the refrigerator, where I found a bag of carrots and some cream cheese. Now, I'm not a cream-cheese person normally, and I don't particularly care for carrots, but seeing as how I was an uninvited guest, I thought it impolite to complain. So I tore into those carrots.

I couldn't have eaten more than half the bag before some tough guy came up to me and said, "Who the hell are you?"

"I'm Bob's friend," I said.

"Who the hell's Bob?" he demanded, raising his voice loud enough to make everyone in the kitchen stop what he was doing to watch.

I just stood there with the "What? Me? What am I doing wrong?" face and made a few indignant snorts to suggest that everyone knew who Bob was.

"Listen, pal," the tough guy said, "I don't know who you are and I don't know any Bob and I'm sure as hell not serving carrots and cream cheese, so I think it's time for you to leave."

The kitchen crowd stood in silence, waiting for my next move. Even though the guy didn't have a walkie-talkie *or* a flashlight, I sensed I was standing on shaky ground. So I did the only thing I could.

I said, "All right. It's your party, so it's your prerogative to invite me to leave. I don't have a problem with that. But" — and I pointed a long, orange carrot with a cream-cheese dollop at his face — "this carrot is coming with me."

I bring all this up because after recently being invited to leave that ultra-hip Deep Ellum dance emporium, The 2826 Club, for doing something as innocuous as taking my pants off so I could more efficiently shake my groove thang, I was beginning to feel unjustly persecuted. I mean, how many times can a guy get invited to leave for absolutely no reason at all? It's ridiculous. I was considering changing my hairstyle to see if that's why it keeps happening.

But then I remembered my father's last visit to town, a mere week before the 2826 Incident. We were in a Speed's at 3 in the morning, shooting pool for $20 a game, when the Old Man decided the Quite Riot song that someone kept playing on the jukebox was becoming tiresome. You can only listen to "Cum on Feel the Noise" six or seven times, with the volume knob set at 11, before your ears start to bleed and you have to ask the manager to turn it down, which the Old Man did. And the manager did turn it down a few notches — for about a minute. Then, for whatever reason, he turned it back up. Louder.

There was only one thing to do, so, naturally, the Old Man took a running start and hurled his pool stick javelin-style at the wall-mounted speaker nearest our table. Even though I explained that my father has an acute sense of hearing and pleaded with the manager to let us stay and finish our game because we were gambling, the Old Man and I were still invited to leave.

Remembering that special father-son moment, I now understand why the guys with walkie-talkies always take such an interest in me. There's nothing I can do about it. Changing my hairstyle won't help. The cause lies much deeper, at the roots. As Hank Jr. says, it's a fam-ly tra-di-shun.

Before Jonathan Melvoin Left Us, We Have Been Told, He Was Having Loads of Fun

HERE AT THE MR. FUNNY GUY INSTITUTE FOR RECREATION, WE LIKE to keep readers abreast of developing amusement trends. When Jarts hit the scene, we were the first to break the news. ("A lawn-dart game the whole family can play!") When poorly aimed Jarts caused the deaths of several children with slow reaction times, we were again the first to warn parents. ("What the hell were we thinking? Lobbing metal spikes around the yard? That can't be wise.")

This week, the Mr. Funny Guy Institute for Recreation continues in its tradition of excellence by bringing you the hottest new amusement fad: heroin! All the kids are doing it. Life stressing you out? Heroin is just the thing to make those troubles go away.

As Lou Reed put it, "When the smack begins to flow, ah, I really don't care anymore about all the Jim-Jims in this town and all the politicians making crazy sounds and everybody putting everybody else down and the dead bodies piled up in mounds."

More research is needed to find out what exactly "Jim-Jims" are and how they affect stress levels, but we can all agree that politicians making crazy sounds is a big problem. And mounds of dead bodies certainly aren't helping any.

By way of clarification, Mr. Reed added, "When that heroin is in my blood and the blood is in my head, man, thank God that I'm good as dead and thank your god that I'm not aware and thank God that I just don't care and I guess I just don't know." Which is precisely our point.

Besides making your troubles go away, heroin can also keep you entertained for hours on end. We at the institute read William S. Burroughs' *Naked Lunch*, a book that helped start the current recreational heroin trend. (The movie, for the kids who don't read much, helped, too.)

Mr. Burroughs wrote: "I had not taken a bath in a year nor changed my clothes or removed them except to stick a needle every hour in the fibrous gray wooden flesh of terminal addiction. I never cleaned nor dusted the room. Empty ampule boxes and garbage piled to the ceiling. ... I did absolutely nothing. I could look at the end of my shoe for eight hours."

What fun! Why go through the hassle of leaving the house to see a movie when you can stay home, shoot up, and watch your shoe for eight hours? No wonder all the hip rock-and-rollers today can't get enough of the stuff. The Red Hot Chili Peppers' Hillel Slovak, Nirvana's Kurt Cobain, Blind Melon's Shannon Hoon, and, most recently, Smashing Pumpkins' Jonathan Melvoin — they all showed us that for those in the know, heroin is the way to go.

As Mr. Melvoin said recently of heroin, "Blurph," and, "Ulk." Then, of course, he died. But before Mr. Melvoin left us, we have been told, he was having loads of fun and wasn't worried one bit about Jim-Jims. Heroin is *that* effective.

And now comes *Trainspotting*, the summer's feel-good hit. "I chose not to choose life," our narrator tells us in the opening moments of *Trainspotting*. "I chose something else. And the reasons? There are no reasons. Who needs reasons when you've got heroin?"

Which brings to mind something Geddy Lee once said: "If you choose not to decide, you still have made a choice." But let's not cloud the issue.

The point is, heroin is hot! Just as Mr. Melvoin's death caused a run on the type of heroin that killed him, so, too, will *Trainspotting* keep smack dealers busy.

However, we at the Mr. Funny Guy Institute for Recreation do have one warning for aspiring heroin users. Just as Jarts had an adverse side effect, so does heroin. It's called withdrawal. We called a friend to ask him about it. He's a recovering addict who used to eat only bread (toasted, otherwise he'd vomit it up) so he'd have enough money for heroin.

"Every heroin user quits once a day," he told the institute. "You go, 'That's it. That was my last one.' Then you get sick. It makes you feel like you have arthritis in every joint in your body. You get stomach cramps and cold sweats. That can last for three or four days, just sitting there, with arthritis and aches and cramps, feeling like a wretch. People call, and you can't even answer the phone."

Luckily, there's an easy solution. "All you have to do," he said, "is find $10 and call your dealer."

Wine Coolers: The Date-Rape Drink

WE MEDIA TYPES ARE SOMETIMES ACCUSED OF SENSATIONALIZING issues and preying on people's fears, so I'll put this as delicately as I can: While you are reading this, pill-pushing thugs are date-raping your innocent daughters.

Sorry. I promised not to do that, and then I went and did it anyway. Now I know how the good-intentioned producers of *Hard Copy* must feel. They're the ones who brought "roofies" to the national consciousness earlier this year. "Roofies," if you haven't heard, is the street name of the sedative Rohypnol, THE VICIOUSLY ADDICTIVE DRUG THAT IS SWEEPING THE COUNTRY LIKE A PLAGUE!

There I go again. I hate myself. It's so hard to stop. IT'S ALMOST AS IF I'M HOOKED ON SOMETHING WORSE THAN ROOFIES!

Except we all know that isn't possible. As *Hard Copy* told us, nothing is worse than roofies — also known as "rope," "roach," and "the forget pill," because, in addition to making users feel fearless and aggressive, roofies can cause blackouts, with total memory loss. That's how the aforementioned pill-pushing thugs have used roofies to date-rape your innocent daughters. The thugs prowl nightclubs, slipping the pills into women's drinks and having sex with them once they have been rendered senseless.

In truth, there have been only a handful of actual roofie-related rapes. Nevertheless, I would like to stress that YOUR WIFE STANDS AN EXCELLENT CHANCE OF DRINKING A ROOFIE-LACED TOM COLLINS AT A TUPPERWARE PARTY AND GETTING RAPED!

If you don't believe me, then you probably don't subscribe to *Time* magazine. Last month, *Time* ran a story titled " 'Roofies': The Date-Rape Drug." The story proclaimed, "Now there's a new risk for women to worry about at parties or bars," and, "… the roofie wave probably hasn't even crested yet. So, experts say, quiz your kids. And don't take your eyes off your drink."

Wait. Have I mentioned ebola yet? A KILLER VIRUS CALLED EBOLA IS POISED TO INFECT THE EARTH'S ENTIRE POPULATION! IT LIQUEFIES YOUR INTERNAL ORGANS AND MAKES YOUR EYEBALLS BLEED, WHICH DOCTORS SAY IS PAINFUL!

Where was I? Oh, yes. Roofies. You mustn't ever take your eyes off your drink. WHATEVER YOU DO, WHEN ATTENDING PARTIES OR PATRONIZING BARS, REMEMBER TO STARE AT YOUR DRINKS!

Now, there are some misguided individuals — so tragically blinded by facts and paralyzed by reason they are! — who would make the outrageous claim that alcohol itself almost certainly plays a role in more date rapes than do roofies. These so-called "thinking" people would suggest that we in the media are perhaps doing the public a disservice when we focus so much attention on roofies. Date rape is our real problem, they contend. Not the substance. If we want to prevent date rapes, these people would tell us, then why not warn young women about the perils of drinking too many wine coolers, which are deceptively sweet yet contain more alcohol than beer?

I'll tell you why: Wine coolers are boring. Everybody's already heard about wine coolers. Remember those two guys sitting on the porch? You know: "We thank you for your support." After that, you want us to write an article titled "Wine Coolers: The Date-Rape Drink"? That's not scary.

Roofies, on the other hand — now *those* are scary. And how about "roach"? That's even better. People hate roaches. MARAUDING MOTORCYCLE GANGS INFECTED WITH EBOLA ARE USING ROACH TO DATE-RAPE YOUR GRANDMOTHERS! Now you're talking newsstand sales.

But don't go hopping into your bathtubs with your toasters. There is one bit of calming news from the roofie war front. Last week, the U.S. Customs Service sealed our border against the evil scourge. While the sale of Rohypnol has always been illicit in the United States, U.S.-bound travelers had been allowed to bring with them a three-month supply for personal use. No more. Customs is now collecting the pills. Smugglers face up to five years in prison and fines up to $10,000.

The scare is over. The danger has passed. Outlawing Rohypnol will no doubt work as well as it has with marijuana. And as it did with alcohol. Your daughters are safe. Breathe easy.

Shoot Anyone Who Drives a Special-Edition Pace Car of Any Make

MODERN LIVING CAN BE SO WACKY AND TOPSY-TURVY. IT'S ENOUGH to drive a body to seek solace in horse tranquilizers. Things used to be simpler. Now we must make difficult decisions on a daily basis.

To paint your breakfast nook with Martha Stewart's Araucana Silkie White or Ralph Lauren's Santa Fe Polo Mallet White? To snack on new olestra-fortified Pringles or new Baked Lay's? To tell your therapist you've been abducted by the space aliens or to keep your mouth shut?

But, judging from reader mail here at the Mr. Funny Guy Centre for Firearms, perhaps no other matter vexes Americans more than uncertainty over the rules and safety guidelines of highway gunplay. I receive letter after letter saying, "Tim, when can I shoot someone in traffic?" Or, "If someone else has already shot a motorist to death, can I shoot the dead motorist's passengers?" Or, "Is it safe to talk on my cellular phone while shooting my pistol out the sun roof?"

Many of you have been asking these questions since a grand jury last month declined to indict Gordon Hale III, who was the first Texan to kill someone with a gun permitted under the new right-to-carry law. You will remember that Mr. III killed a man in an altercation that erupted after a minor traffic accident — right here in Dallas, where we teach 'em to shoot at presidents and at people who shoot at presidents.* Mr. III's non-indictment, you all understand, paves the way to safer transportation through the use of handguns.

Your questions have all been excellent. They demonstrate that you Texans are intelligent, reasonable people who only lack a little direction, vis-à-vis where to aim your gunfire. So, this week, as a service to all my readers, I will outline the Official Rules for Vehicular Gunplay.

Rule No. 1: Remember never to mix alcohol and firearms. While a 40-ounce bottle of St. Ides malt-liquor beverage might make for an otherwise enjoyably dizzy Sunday-afternoon drive, it will adversely affect your marksmanship.

Many motorists say, "I shoot straighter after I've had a few drinks," but that simply is not the case. Similarly, if you are taking one or more prescription drugs, including "roofies," "cat," "ice," or "smack," or if you are a recreational user of the over-the-counter cough syrup Robitussin, then leave your guns in your glove compartments.

Rule No. 2: All firearms should be treated as if they are loaded. Never point a gun at anything unless you are prepared to deal with the consequences of destroying it. The only exception to this rule is when you know for *certain* a gun isn't loaded — or at least *strongly suspect* it isn't loaded. If you're pretty sure a gun isn't loaded, it's okay to wave it in the air while you drive. This will create around your vehicle what's known as a "cushion of safety."

Rule No. 3: Always keep your finger off the trigger until you're ready to shoot. When it comes time to cap someone's ass, though, like if some motherfucker pulls some crazy-ass shit on the road and turns without signaling, then hold your gat sideways and thrust it forward with each shot, saying, "You want some of this? I got yours right here!"

Rule No. 4: Think first. Shoot second. Drive third.

Rule No. 5: If two drivers, traveling in perpendicular directions, arrive simultaneously at an intersection controlled by a four-way stop, and if those two drivers then see someone who deserves a cap in his ass, the second driver, counting clockwise, gets to take the first shot. If he misses, the first driver not only gets to shoot the original target but also has the option of shooting the second driver.

Rule No. 6: Never discharge your handgun while talking on a cellular phone. If you see another motorist talking on a cellular phone, waste him.

Rule No. 7: Shoot anyone who drives a special-edition pace car of any make.

Rule No. 8: By state law, the driver who hits another car from behind is always at fault. So have your gun at the ready, should you be rear-ended. If you ever rear-end someone, prepare to return fire.

Rule No. 9: If you arrive at the scene of a gun battle in progress, take note of both caliber and number of weapons involved, then shoot at whomever has the most firepower. This will even the odds.

Rule No. 10: Fire friendly!

*From Rev. Ivan Stang

16

Then My Friends Drew All Over My Face With Lipstick Liner

I HATE OKLAHOMA. I MEAN, I HATE IT WITH A RIGHTEOUS FURY OF BIB-lical proportions. I hate everything about that damn state. I hate Indian bingo. I hate Rodgers, and I hate Hammerstein! I'll tell you why.

In honor of the brave Americans who died fighting for our free-dom — probably none of whom were from Oklahoma — I went to Lake Murray, which is located in Oklahoma, to get drunk and oper-ate high-speed watercraft. This is why we have Memorial Day. Our forefathers threw themselves under Hitler's panzers trying to hold the Maginot line or whatever so that every right-minded American could have the opportunity to get loaded to the gills at the lake and ride a Jet Ski.

So we were out on a friend's houseboat, about 10 of us, drinking Keystone Light. I don't know how we wound up with a cooler full of Keystone Light, but that's what we had. And the idea at the lake is to tie up to a buoy in a cove and basically just float and drink what-ever happens to be in your cooler, which, as I said, was Keystone Light. And because there aren't enough buoys to go around on a crowded Memorial Day, you have to share. Folks come up and say howdy and tie their boat to yours, and there's not much you can really do about it besides sit there and float and say howdy back. If you're a single man — and pretty much if you're a married man, too — you hope that the boat that ties up to yours is full of 18-year-old, bikini-clad Swedish girls.

The boat that wound up docking next to ours was skippered by a fat, mustachioed man who had a poorly drawn tattoo of the Playboy bunny on his right breast. His little buddy was a one-legged guy who spoke a dialect of Oklahoma English that linguists have yet to decode. He was always saying something to the effect of, "Boy howdy, oz gun justay at thouse, buh thin, shit, lack to be so damn ot ain't ne'er ane seen nun at for," and I'd just go, "I know what you're saying, man," and laugh. Rocking boats are a bitch on one-legged guys, though. He fell down a couple times, which proved that slapstick comedy bridges all cultural boundaries.

But so that's how the day went, without complication. I sat on the deck of the houseboat, drinking Keystone Light and turning magenta, while waiting for the one-legged guy to fall down. There was one tense moment when My Fair Lady asked me, "Do the backs of my legs look like cottage cheese?" But the backs of her legs don't look anything like cottage cheese, so a potentially ugly situation was easily avoided. It was all smooth floating. Until I noticed something unusual.

Around 5 o'clock, I began to sense a profound bloatedness. By then, I had put away — I don't know — maybe a dozen Keystone Lights. My belly, now sunburned so badly that it was the same color as my nipples, was beginning to hurt. And I could feel it hurt. Which meant I wasn't drunk. Just as I was coming to this realization, I heard someone say, "We really should have brought some beer with us from Texas. This three-two Oklahoma stuff just doesn't do the trick."

It was then that I blued the air with such profanity that was unfit for the ears of fair women. Even the Playboy skipper and his one-legged little buddy seemed offended.

I will not pretend to understand the volumetric principles underlying "three-two" beer. I thought it meant the beer was only 3.2 percent alcohol, as opposed to Texas' 6 percent, but someone said he had a friend who worked for Budweiser and that his Budweiser friend told him that 3.2 beer isn't all that different from normal beer, that the 3.2 designation had something to do with how they weigh beer in Oklahoma and was not a true measure of alcohol content.

Whatever. All I knew was I wasn't drunk. And my sunburn was really starting to sting. And I blamed Oklahoma. Thank God we had a bottle of vodka in the freezer. I immediately poured myself about nine fingers of McCormick. If you've never had McCormick, it isn't exactly your top-shelf vodka. We didn't have any ice cubes, so I stuck a Popsicle in it to keep it cold. In the space of an hour, I think I had one purple McCormick, one orange, and one red. Then I took off all my clothes and did *Waterworld* stunts on the Jet Ski. Then I went below deck on the houseboat and passed clear out. Then my friends drew all over my face with lipstick liner.

All of which could have been avoided if they didn't sell such anemic beer in Oklahoma and I didn't have to overcompensate. But I make you this solemn promise: You won't catch me in that cursed land again unprepared. Next time I'm bringing my own beer.

Understand That This Was No Ordinary Bar

EVERY MAN MEASURES HIS LIFE AND THE PATH HE TAKES IN IT WITH A more or less similar wagonful of milestones. As a tot, he learns to ride a bicycle. Knowingly or not, he marks that moment, mentally, with a stone. Up till then, his domain was limited by where his feet could take him; now he has wheels.

Later, as a lad, he proves he can parallel-park and gets his driver's license. He tastes his first beer. Then he smokes his first reefer. Marijuana, old Mary Jane, she's a gateway drug, as we all know, and soon enough our young man moves on to crank, ice, bennies, flakes, horse, and whatever else is currently on the market in Plano. Each substance another milestone.

Add to this list of significant events in every man's life the occasion on which, seated with his colleagues in a bar, his entrepreneurial spirit buoyed by gin martinis, he opens his mouth and utters these words: "Hey, we could buy this place!"

Thus spoke I on a recent Thursday evening while exercising the old elbow at a Lower Greenville bar. Rather than a cock crow (signaling my betrayal of common sense), I heard a thud. That was the milestone hitting the path. Dirt path, it appears.

Actually, I can't claim for certain that I first spoke those words. It might have been another in our group who initially hit upon the idea and said, "Hey, we could buy this place!" But I was only a short step behind, and I put my own spin on the notion by adding, "Hey, we *could* buy this place! Fucking A!"

(Major aside: I have always wanted to own (but not actually operate, because my hands are tender) a ranch whose brand would be the "Fucking A." You know, like the "Running W" or whatever. My brand would look like this .)

Now, we had some assistance in giving birth to this buy-the-bar idea. You could say the bartender (and owner) was our midwife. To protect his identity, I'll call him Mr. Z. As previously mentioned, some of Mr. Z's assistance was mixed with dry vermouth. The remainder of it, though, he served straight up, when one of our number innocently remarked that, for a Thursday night, the place did not appear to enjoy a surfeit of paying customers and, in fact, had seemed that way since it opened about five months earlier.

"Boys," Mr. Z told us, "I'll tell you the truth. Business has been bad. I'm selling the place this weekend."

At first, we couldn't process what we'd heard. "Sell the bar? But how can you serve us drinks if you sell the bar?" Then it hit us, the full force of the tragedy. We pulled out our own hair. We rent our clothes. Not since Hecuba gave voice to her sorrow as Achilles dragged the lifeless body of her son, Hector, behind his well-built chariot has such wailing been heard.

Understand that this was no ordinary bar. No, it was far more than that. This was a place that inspired loyalty of the sort that is more commonly found on battlefields and at Microsoft. One afternoon, for example, after a hard day of staring at computer screens, a co-worker and I stopped in to visit Mr. Z. He had our preferred cocktails in front of us, without our having to ask for them, almost precisely as our butts alighted on the barstools. Whereupon my chum asked, with total and complete sincerity, "Is it right to love a bar the same way you, like, love a woman?" It was that kind of place.

So when Mr. Z broke the news, and when he further revealed the six-figure bid that we'd have to top if we really wanted to own the joint, we got to confabulating. Being "content providers," all of us, we didn't have the roll to buy the bar, but we knew people who did. Attorneys. Record-label moguls. Well-coiffed playboy restaurateurs.

"I play poker with this guy who's loaded," one of us said. Another (perhaps me) offered, "I read this article a couple months back in *P.O.V.* or *Maxim* or the *New Republic* called 'How to Own a Bar.' I think it was in the same issue with 'How to Throw a Punch' and 'How to Screw for Hours.' "

We cadged a cell phone from another patron and called potential investors, asking them to drop by and check the place out. Keep in mind that this was close to midnight. Technically, then, I believe we were making bootie calls. How embarrassing.

The next day, of course, in harsh light unfiltered by barroom blinds, far more sober, we still wanted to buy the place. Unquestionably it was a bully idea. But our rich friends had, by then, instructed their secretaries to inform us they weren't in. I am afraid to stop in and ask Mr. Z (if he's there), but I assume the bar has been sold.

I have hit another milestone and passed it. Before that fateful evening, life was laden with possibility. Owning a bar. Hitting an unboxed superfecta in the last race at Lone Star Park. Getting stuck in a well-ventilated elevator with tennis sensation Martina Hingis and scoring a casual blowjob. It all could happen.

Now I know better. There is hope, sure. But not for me.

The Treacherous Snake and His Tasty Pies

ONCE UPON A TIME, IN AN AREA NOT SO VERY DISTANT, THERE LIVED a treacherous, evildoing snake. His name was Robert or Matthew. Something like that. It's not important. And the treacherous, evildoing area snake was an accomplished cook. Very handy in the kitchen, this snake.

The literal-minded might well wonder how a snake, an animal obviously lacking hands — and arms, too — could possibly be handy in the kitchen. And the literal-minded can go screw themselves. This was no ordinary treacherous, evildoing snake. Not only could he cook without the aid of hands or arms, but he was a formidable kegler. He had no equal in the area, and his mantelshelf sagged under the weight of his many shiny trophies, which he polished compulsively. Without hands.

Right. So the treacherous, evildoing snake was a mean cook. And though he was more than proficient in every discipline within the culinary arts, pies were his specialty. Cherry pies, apple pies, chestnut pies, Key lime pies, pecan pies, lemon meringue pies — each one more scrumptious than the next. So delicious were his pies and so coveted were they by the other area animals that the snake quit his regular job as a data-systems analyst and opened a pie shop.

The treacherous, evildoing, pie-baking area snake prospered. His bank account (and his appellative) grew.

As it happened, one pie, the rhubarb pie, in fact, outsold the others by a wide margin. Area pie-loving animals agreed that the snake's rhubarb pie was the tastiest pie they had ever eaten. They queued up to buy the snake's rhubarb pie. Many reported that their day wasn't complete without some of the snake's rhubarb pie. They enjoyed a piece after every meal and said it gave them a sense of well-being.

One day in the snake's shop, a hungry monkey who craved the rhubarb pie asked the snake, "What do you put in your rhubarb pie that makes it so irresistibly delicious, so alive with pleasure?"

"That," answered the snake, "I cannot tell you. A secret ingredient gives my rhubarb pie its special flavor, and if I told you, other bakers in the area might copy my recipe and drive me out of business."

The hungry monkey said he understood and, rhubarb pie in hand, went on his way.

But something odd happened. Area pie-loving animals began to fall ill. They came down with apnea and dyspnea, high blood pressure and low blood pressure, coughing and cachexia. Not to mention nasty nasal discharge and death. The situation grew so dire that area officials finally stepped in to investigate the snake's shop and his pie-baking procedure.

An official donkey asked the snake, "Is there anything you put in your pies, specifically the popular rhubarb pie, that might cause coughing and cachexia. Not to mention nasty nasal discharge and death?"

"Absolutely not," answered the snake. "I simply bake the tastiest pies I can. Care for a piece?"

"I'll pass," said the donkey, and he asked to borrow the snake's fax machine so he could fax in his official report.

As it happened, the treacherous, evildoing snake owned a very fancy fax machine paid for with his pie profits, one featuring a convenient memory function. Thinking on his hooves, the official donkey printed the contents of the fax machine's memory. In among the snake's recently faxed documents, the donkey found a copy of the recipe for the snake's rhubarb pie.

The recipe called for these ingredients: sugar, flour, butter, rhubarb, and "a delicious, secret flavoring agent that is highly addictive and leads, inexorably, to the death of the pie eater (alas)."

"Aha!" cried the official donkey. "Just as I suspected. You've known all along that your popular rhubarb pies are killing area animals. And yet you continued to sell them and prosper. No wonder they call you a treacherous, evildoing snake."

To punish the snake, the official donkey hired a pack of litigious wolves to sue the snake for compensation for the rise in health-care costs resulting from the poisonous, though tasty, rhubarb pies. And the wolves won. The snake agreed to pay $206 billion over a period of 25 years. It was the largest civil settlement in the area's history.

"This will teach that snake," said the donkey at a press conference announcing the settlement. "We'll use this money to educate area animals and improve area roads. Or we'll build a new sports arena. Whatever."

But instead of closing his shop or discontinuing his line of rhubarb pies or even omitting the secret ingredient, the treacherous, evildoing snake simply raised the price of a pie 45 cents to pay off the settlement.

At first, the area monkey complained about the price increase. But then he grew hungry and bought another rhubarb pie.

The end.

Texturized Nylon Doesn't Do Well When Exposed to Direct Fire

SOME THINGS — THROWING UP, FOR INSTANCE — ALWAYS SEEM funny the next day. Or, if it's not funny the next day, due to a hangover so grievous that you'd end it all by strangling yourself with your shoelaces had you not been required to remove them during the booking process, then certainly throwing up is funny by the second day or, at the very latest, the third day. Even lousy friends will bail you out by the third day. Shouldn't they?

But then there are other things — I'm thinking, specifically, about the fight one of my best friends recently picked with me — that will never seem funny and that call for the cultivation of righteous hatred and a mean payback. I was thinking about sleeping with his wife to get even, but that would only relieve him of the duty. Now I'm thinking about his daughter.

Area readers have met the man of whom I speak. They know him as Beric. He who frets excessively over the size of his monster ass. He who will not hesitate, while riding as a passenger in my car, to hawk phlegm into various onboard periodicals.

As it happened, Beric and I served together in a bachelor party posse last weekend. In the early going, the party was rolling along just fine. Thanks to the kind people at Three Ring Limousine (if you think that's a shameless plug, talk to Beric's daughter in a few weeks), we were barhopping in style. Even our able driver, Larry, could not have foreseen the trouble ahead.

It started over my alleged low level of party participation. The facts: We were on the third stop in our tour, already well fortified with vodka and hopped up on pornographic videos screened in the limo (check out *Clown Fuckers* if you get a chance). A fellow party-goer and I got involved in what I'm sure was an important conversation, possibly about Troy Aikman's clavicle. We became momentarily separated from the group.

Beric stumbled up to me, malice in his eyes, and said, "Stop hanging out by yourself, dude. Get over here with the rest of party."

Then he went too far. Beric said, "You think you're too cool for school."

Nobody calls me too cool for school.

I explained to Beric exactly how mistaken he was, bolstering my point with a reference to his mother's sexual proclivities and his involvement therein, and I turned to walk away. That's when Beric kicked my ass. Literally. In the right buttock.

I spun around and manfully threw my lit cigar at him. The business end of the stogie exploded in a shower of incandescent ash, but Beric was unharmed. He made a move toward me. I puffed up my chest and told Beric, "You want some of this? You want some? You don't want to mess with this." All the while, retreating.

To be honest, I didn't like my chances. I had the reach on Beric. In a boxing ring, I would take him. But a bar fight is an altogether different matter. You've got punching mixed with grappling, plus endemic objects, such as chairs and bottles, that come into play. And you do not want to lose a fight a friend. You lose a fight to a stranger and, as long as you gave it the college try, you can live with yourself.

"At least I kicked him in the crotch before he beat me up," you can say.

"Hell of a shot to the crotch," your friends will say.

Your wounds will heal, because you'll never see the guy. But if you lose a fight to a friend, he'll kick your ass all over again every time you see him — mentally.

"How's it going?" you'll ask him.

"Fine," he'll say. "Remember that time I kicked your ass?"

I like to think that Beric found himself faced with the same dilemma and couldn't decide for certain which of us would take the title. Rather than escalate the confrontation, he threw his cigar at me. I would have taken the hit as well as Beric, except I was wearing a shirt made of texturized nylon, and texturized nylon doesn't do well when exposed to direct fire. I managed to put out the shirt and save all six of my chest hairs.

Many men — especially many men who had spent the better part of an afternoon removing the buttons from a texturized nylon shirt and installing faux mother-of-pearl snap fasteners — would have pouted for the rest night and repeatedly told the other partygoers, "Look what Beric did to my shirt," and, "I installed these snaps myself." Not me. I redoubled my drinking efforts and began planning my revenge. The next day, I was not laughing.

Bodily Functions

I Used to Think the Bidet Was a Morally Corruptive Device Best Left to the French

BECAUSE I AM ACUTELY HIP, THE OTHER DAY I WAS IDLING AWAY time in a coffeehouse, reading about how to get my chakras all spinning at the same speed by performing Tibetan rites, when suddenly the iced mocha kicked in. Just as liquor loosens lips, so do caffeinated beverages similarly affect the bowels.

Now, as a general rule, I try to manage my schedule so as never to have to sit down in a foreign restroom. I have a fear of using unfamiliar facilities. It comes from having attended K.B. Polk elementary school, where, at least during my tenure, male students took great pleasure in tormenting anyone on a toilet.

I once made the terrible mistake of moving my bowels at K.B. Polk. The other boys stood on the johns in the stalls next to mine and looked down on me, asking rude questions like, "Having fun in there?" And, "Hey, buddy, you layin' some pipe?" Then they threw wet toilet paper at me.

The experience traumatized me so severely that I never again put myself in that vulnerable position while at school. No matter how desperately I might have needed to go, I waited until I got home and could operate in the safety of my own bathroom.

With one ignoble exception, I was able to keep my intestines in check. One day, we were playing a game called "Smear the Queer" (political correctness had not yet come to K.B. Polk) that involved a wad of notebook paper and full-contact tackling. The object was to run around the schoolyard with the paper wad and avoid getting the snot beaten out of you.

On that particular day, I had been struggling mightily to contain myself, but, experiencing a temporary drop in pressure, I grabbed the wad and ran with it. I moved like Billy Simms, juking and dodging through the schoolyard on what would have been the afternoon's finest run, if not for Matt Freeman's vicious blindside. He put a lick on me that rattled my teeth and made my eyes well up. It also knocked the crap out of me. Literally.

Still, to this day, I would rather risk soiling my pants than use an alien bathroom and face possible harassment. K.B. Polk scarred me that deeply.

But then I found myself last week in that coffeehouse called Java

Jones, all jicked up on iced mocha, reading about the chakra-spinning Tibetan rites, and I felt a disturbance in my pipes. I had plenty more time to idle away and was feeling unusually brave, so I girded myself for action and found the head.

Simply put, my visit to Java Jones' bathroom was the most wondrous eliminatory experience I've had in weeks — possibly months. The kind folks at Java Jones keep the lights low in their bathroom, and the wallpaper, a Mercator-projection map of the Earth, gives the place a soothing blue hue that makes you feel like you're under water.

But the best part about Java Jones' bathroom is the toilet, which isn't really a toilet at all. It's a bidet. Having never utilized one, I used to think the bidet was a morally corruptive appliance best left to the French. Now I've reconsidered.

The seat on this machine at Java Jones heats up, putting even the most tense of recta at ease. Just like Captain Picard's chair on the bridge of the *Enterprise,* a control panel with an array of buttons sits at your right hand. At your command are two cleansing streams of heated water, one for the "back" and one for the "front." You can adjust the force of each. A refreshing blow-dryer finishes the job. What you've got here is highly advanced lavatory technology.

Here I must remind you that I'm a trained writer. In putting this rig through its paces, by testing its operational limits, I was merely doing my job. When I tell you that I sat in the bathroom at Java Jones for upwards of 15 minutes, giggling and fiddling with all the buttons, searching for the optimal stream setting, I want you to understand that I was practicing good journalism. It was my responsibility to find out if the thing was safe and also to see if anyone would try to throw wet toilet paper at me while I was using it.

I can report that the Java Jones clientele respects privacy, and the bidet is safe. Caffeine technician Laurie Lyon, who handcrafted my iced mocha, told me that they work hard to provide a secure bathroom environment. Although, she said, one lady monopolized the bidet for so long that the fire department had to be called in to break open the bathroom door with the jaws of life and forcibly remove her from the appliance (lie).

Laurie also told me something else of interest: There are two Java Jones locations, and the other one has a bidet, too. More research is obviously needed. Don't worry. I'm on top of it.

Editor's note: Sadly, the bidet was not enough to ensure Java Jones' survival when Starbucks came to town.

According to My Research, Even Jesus Christ Farted

WE WERE STANDING IN THE KITCHEN WHEN IT HAPPENED. PRESENT were my fiancée, her parents, and I. We were discussing the upcoming holidays and our impending marriage, and we were drinking coffee, which might have had something to do with it.

It is important to understand that I cherish my future in-laws. They are genuinely good, caring people. They are one of the reasons, after years of swearing (and wagering) I'd never marry, that I finally broke down and bought a diamond. I will one day be proud to call them, if not Mom and Dad, then at least by their first names.

But my future in-laws, God bless them, are somewhat strait-laced. They're Republicans, and they play golf. Which isn't to say they're bores. They're simply genteel, dignified folk.

That is why I was caught off guard when we were standing in the kitchen, making wedding plans, and my future mother-in-law farted. Just using that term in a sentence referring to her makes me uncomfortable. The sound came from my left, where she was standing, and, though it was but a meek, piccolo noise, it so startled me that I nearly leapt.

A lesser woman might have pretended nothing happened, but my future mother-in-law, demonstrating enormous composure even while experiencing technical difficulties, said, "Excuse me." I thought for a moment about saying, "Bless you," or cracking a joke about the strength of the coffee but decided in the end to keep quiet.

Later, after I bade farewell to my in-laws and had some time to reflect on the kitchen incident, I realized that the significance of the event could not be overestimated. It explains why my betrothed and I take such disparate approaches to flatulence — and bodily functions in general. Because while nature largely determines the tenor of our farts, nurture dictates how we deal with them, and with an understanding of our upbringing come clues to our future.

Myself, I was raised by farters. My mother is a prodigious farter. She'd break wind in church if she thought she could pull it off anonymously. My father never goes to church, but I think he is the actual boogie-woogie bugle boy of Company C of whom the Andrews sisters sang. He taught me at an early age about the elusive species of arachnid known as the barking spider.

So, naturally, I grew up to be a farter. In all but the most formal of settings, I won't hesitate to let loose the nether zephyr. My fiancée, on the other hand, was reared by parents with a more heightened sense of decorum. She claims she never farts, that she in fact lacks the capacity to do so.

I know this to be false. I did some actual fart research on the Internet and learned that everyone, without exception, passes gas between 10 and 15 times per day. (I also learned that most birds, fishes, and insects also fart; that the No. 1 question received by the children's television show *Beakman's World* was "Where do farts come from?"; and that Joseph Pujol, a French "fartiste" who died in 1945, became so internationally famous for his fart-singing and comedy farting routines that a street in Paris was named after him.) According to my research, even Jesus Christ farted. He was like man in every respect except that he could not commit sin, and, though I don't recall covering the subject in my catechism classes, I doubt farting is a sin, so He must have done it.

An examination along these lines leads to the aforementioned clues about what the future may hold for the bride and me. If we assume the maximum daily number of farts per person, 15, then there exists a 62.5 percent chance the average person will fart in any given hour. If we also assume our wedding will last one hour and that 300 people will be in attendance, then 187.5 people will either fart or feel the urge to fart in church, during the actual ceremony.

If we further assume that the night before the wedding, at the rehearsal dinner, I will imbibe a reasonable yet statistically significant 5.8 beers, followed by perhaps one high-priced cognac, and if we assume that on the wedding day itself, I will be feeling the aftereffects of those beverages — combined with the gastrointestinal stress that attends vowing to love someone till death do you part — then chances are good I'll be among the 187.5.

I'm sure the Almighty — and my mother-in-law — will understand.

"And What Color Is Your Urine?"

"**G**OOD MORNING. THIS IS PAM. IS YOUR QUESTION ABOUT YOURSELF?"
"Yes."

"Have you ever called here before?"

"Oh, yeah."

"So you know we're all nurses, and we ask questions about symptoms of illness or injury and make recommendations about safe levels of care?"

"Sure."

"Go ahead."

"I've actually got three questions about stuff that has been ... uh ... plaguing me. The first one is, I have a bump on my back. It's not inflamed or anything, and it doesn't hurt to push on it, but my wife keeps telling me I need to go to the dermatologist to have it excised."

"And how long have you had that bump?"

"Probably a month or two. But the only time it's really ever an issue is when I'm getting a back scratch and she says something about it."

"It's non-painful and non-red?"

"Check. Non-painful whatsoever. Also non-red. Non-colored, in fact. I just told her that it's probably a sebaceous cyst and no big deal."

"That's one possibility, but I need to ask you some questions about that bump. [Multifarious follow-up questions: Is the bump festering? Positive you don't have any kind of retained foreign body, like a splinter?] Well, it's pretty hard to tell what it might be. I recommend that you see your primary-care physician in the next two weeks. I can make a referral."

"My next question — and I've put these in order of least- to most-hypochondriacal sounding — is about my tongue, which, for the past two weeks, has felt sort of fat. And that's not 'phat' with a 'ph.' "

"Like swollen?"

"Yeah. Also, when I touch my teeth with it, it feels almost numb. And along the sides of it, it's raw. I've looked at it in the mirror, and it looks almost white."

"Both sides or one?"

"Both."

"You haven't had any trauma in your mouth, have you?"

"Not that I can recall."

"Is this lesion painful?"

"I wouldn't call it a lesion."

"Whatever it is, does it hurt?"

"I wouldn't say hurt. Tender is maybe as far as I'd go, like I'm wearing a sweater on my tongue. It's like I've burned it, except I haven't. And I want to assure you that I'm pretty fastidious when it comes to oral hygiene. Is this just a common thing that can pop up if you have a cold? I've got one."

"No. It's not. [nervous chuckle] I'm going to recommend again that you see your doctor in the next two weeks. You said you had a third problem?"

"Yeah. So now we venture into a more personal realm. It seems like, in the past year maybe, I've had to get up at night more frequently to go to the bathroom. And I forget how this came up, but my wife was telling a friend how I keep waking her up when I have to go to the bathroom, and that person said he had a relative with diabetes, and that was the first sign, getting up at night to urinate."

"I don't know if that would be the first sign. But one symptom of diabetes would be excessive thirst, never feeling satisfied in terms of thirst, and having copious amounts of urine — all around the clock. How often do you have to get up at night to go to the bathroom?"

"Just once. That usually takes care of it."

"Do you have any burning or pain with urination?"

"No."

"Is it a normal flow?"

"Well, I haven't observed a large sample group of different flows, so I'm not sure. Seems normal enough."

"You're not bed-wetting or wetting your underwear?"

"Oh, no."

"And what color is your urine?"

"I guess it depends on what I've been eating and drinking. Asparagus makes it green, and beets make it red. That always scares me at first, but then I go, 'Oh, yeah. Beets.' "

"Basically, when you call your doctor to make an appointment [nervous chuckle], write it down on a piece paper so you don't forget to mention that, so you can discuss these issues."

"Great. I'll write it down so I don't forget."

"Okay. Well, take care of yourself."

"Tell Me When to Stop," She Said.

THERE ARE THOSE, I'M SURE, WHO WOULD CONTEND THAT I GOT A colonic last week just so I could satisfy my scatological need to write about my ass. Those people are assholes.

As Bernard Jensen says, "By making believe the bowel doesn't exist, many people have gone down the path of improper living, treating the bowel indiscriminately and reaping the sad harvest in later years." I have no idea who Bernard Jensen is, but his words haunted me after I stumbled across them on the Web site of a local colon-irrigation firm called Genesis.

Had I been treating my colon indiscriminately? And, if so, what did this "reaping the sad harvest" business entail? I'm not an especially industrious farmer, I'll admit. I'm not saying I deserve an *ecstatic* harvest. I'd settle for happy. But there was Bernard Jensen, suggesting that, due to improper living — which presumably included binge-drinking and staying up till all hours of the night and harboring a serious hatred for Adele Lanan, the only woman who has ever fired me — my happy harvest might never come to pass.

When I discovered that Genesis was conveniently located just down the street from my house, I knew it was time to get back on the path to proper living.

I arrived for my appointment at the converted house in the M Streets area and was greeted by Karen Fahey, the proprietress. If you've met my grandmother, Karen looked a little like her. Only my grandmother doesn't wear blue scrubs. Karen's philosophy, as stated on her Web site, is "Get the old stuff out before you put in the new," which is fortuitous, given Karen's line of work. Like, it would be unfortunate if her philosophy were "Measure twice, cut once."

Karen led me to the bathroom and kindly asked that I take off my clothes. She handed me a blue sheet, with which I was to cover my monstrous Richard (my words) once supine on the table in an adjacent room, the colonatorium (again, my word). This I did.

The colonatorium was dimly lit and painted a pastel plum, no doubt intended to put recta at ease. Various crystals hung by monofilament line in a raised, venetian-blinded window. Beside the foot of the table sat the machine, the cause of not only rectal tension but, in my case at least, cecal apprehension, plus sigmoid panic. My cheeks clench up even now, typing its name: the Electro-Tox 9000. (Actually, it was just called the Electro-Tox. I have taken the liberty of adding the 9000 part because it sounds cooler.)

Karen came in, pulled up a chair, and explained the procedure. Her tableside manner was direct, if a tad phlegmier than I like. Karen had a nasty cold and suffered periodic, incapacitating coughing fits. We've all been there, but I wondered what would happen if Karen fell into such a fit as she worked her index finger into my anus to check for polyps. If she covered her mouth with her free hand, I feared how far her busy finger might accidentally sink. If the reverse happened, then ick. She finished the exam, thankfully, without incident.

Next, we moved on to the colonic proper. Karen produced a hose. One end was attached to the Electro-Tox 9000; the other, with plenty of lubricant, was attached to me. On the latter intromission, I will say this: You gay men are insane. Maybe I'm missing something here. I don't know. But the Electro-Tox 9000 convinced me to keep all my platonic homosexual relationships the way they are.

Turning a knob on the randy machine, Karen slowly filled my colon with warm water. "Tell me when to stop," she said. "Just say, 'Okay, full.' You'll know when." I did. She shut off the water and let me drain, expertly working a vibrating hand massager into my abdomen to help things along. We watched the contents of my colon float through an illuminated translucent tube on the Electro-Tox 9000. Karen cheerfully pointed out the sights like a guide on a riverboat ride at a theme park built for *Escherichia coli*.

"Stuff can sit around in your colon for up to 20 years," she said. I recalled what I had to eat in 1978 but didn't see any Big League Chew go by.

When I was empty, we did it all over again. Rinse, repeat. For about 45 minutes. I at first felt compelled to chat, and we somehow got to talking about Howard Stern. I told Karen how much I liked him and she told me how much she despised him and, seeing as how she was the one at the controls of the Electro-Tox 9000, I shut up for the remainder of the procedure.

When all was said and plumbed, I felt like a new man — a very *empty* new man. Definitely back on the path to proper living and a happy harvest. I would say my path leads back to Genesis but for two reasons: 1) Karen charges $50 per visit, which is a tad dear, and 2) forgetting her warning on my way home, I tried to break wind and instead shat in my pants, which was a tad messy.

My Nipples Performed Exactly As Arden Said They Would

WHEN I WAS A YOUNG LAD, STRUGGLING THROUGH PUBERTY, every new follicle of body hair was cause for celebration. At summer camp, where we had communal showers and I couldn't hide my nether prairie, the other boys used to call me "the bald wonder."

My situation wasn't helped any by my armpits. Hair, thankfully, had begun to take root in that region, but only in my right armpit. The left side lagged behind for some reason, giving me a freakish asymmetry. I kept my arms down as much I could in the shower. This made it hard to wash the hair on my head.

How ironic, then, that I grew up to be a man with hairy nipples. Mother Nature is a cruel gardener. She saw to it that my body hair filled in nicely everywhere a lad would want it, but she couldn't stop herself from adding a little decorative flourish. Although my chest is almost completely bare, hair sprouts from the edge of my areolae. Long, black hairs. Hairs like spider legs reaching for my navel.

That's no good. Naturally, I pluck them. There can be nothing sexier than the sight of a grown man standing shirtless in front of the bathroom mirror, pinching his tit with his left hand, tweezing with his right. Why Michelangelo chose not to sculpt David in that pose, I'll never understand.

So when I heard about a new place in town called Spa Thira that uses high-tech lasers to more or less permanently remove unwanted body hair, I got on the horn. When I heard that a one-time treatment of my "chest area," as they called it, would run about $500, I mentioned that I'm a journalist. To all the poor people out there suffering from hirsutism, I strongly recommend becoming a journalist. The Spa Thira folks set me up an appointment.

The first thing I noticed about the place was that it's a lot nicer than my house. Classical music and the sound of babbling water wafted through the air. The decor was done in shades of white, none of which were probably named "white." I imagine the walls were something like "Amish linen," the carpet "egg shell," the furniture "bleached chicken bone."

The second thing I noticed was that I talk really loud. Michelle, the Spa Thira manager who did my consultation, explained that everyone at Spa Thira speaks in a "spa voice." To me, it sounded like the spa women — I didn't see a single spa man — were all conducting phone sex on a cell phone in church. Theirs were breathy, alluring voices. Michelle made talking about hair removal sound almost erotic.

After my consultation, I was led to my private changing room, which had a vase filled with fresh flowers in it. There I donned a thick, white, comfy terry-cloth robe and flip-flops. "It is the ultimate expression of Spa Thira's skin-care philosophy that beauty should be a revelation, never an ordeal," the Spa Thira brochure said. Here is the revelation I had: If I could, I'd never wear anything but thick, comfy terry-cloth robes.

Then it was off to have my nipples zapped in the laser room, where I lay on a padded table and took off my robe (they provided me a wraparound terry-cloth skirt thing, too). Before the actual zapping could take place, Arden, an "aesthetician," first had to wax my nipples and spread thereupon Spa Thira's "exclusive light-absorbing lotion," which I preferred to call "secret sauce," because Aesthetician Arden said she wasn't allowed to tell me what was in it. It looked and felt like eye black. If I had been shirtless and at bat, I would have had no trouble with glare coming off my nipples.

In any case, Aesthetician Arden compared my nipples to cars. The rings of secret sauce surrounding my areolae would absorb the laser's heat like a black car absorbs the sun's heat. My white skin, like a white car, would remain cool and unaffected.

My nipples performed exactly as Arden said they would. A nurse came in and zapped my teats with a "SoftLight," a low-wattage, neodymium-yttrium-aluminum garnet laser. It hurt less than the waxing, which, if you're alone in a room with a pretty aesthetician, is kind of a turnon. When it was over, Arden gave me a foot massage, a little bonus Spa Thira offers each of its guests. So that was nice.

My whole Spa Thira experience was delightful. As the brochure said, "You emerge renewed and transformed, your skin a pleasure to see and touch, your inner self revealed." Here is what my inner self was wondering: "What's the big deal with body hair? Why not just have it all removed?" And, more importantly, "Would Aesthetician Arden dig the bald wonder?"

Something Went Awry in My Alimentary Canal

BIG NEWS: ECLIPSING ALL PREVIOUS SCIENTIFIC BREAKTHROUGHS, including the formulation of the smallpox vaccine and the discovery that two heads are better than one, snack-food engineers have invented the fat-free, full-taste potato chip. Now health-conscious snackers can snack like it's 1999.

Naturally, there might be side effects. Snack-food engineers accomplished their fat-free feat by frying potato and tortilla chips in a new space-age substance known as olestra, a sugar- and vegetable-based molecule too big for the human digestive system to process, thereby passing through the body without adding fat. The potential complications arise from this "passing through" process. Because of olestra's laxative properties, the FDA has required the snack packaging to carry a warning label that reads, in part: "Olestra may cause abdominal cramping and loose stools." Oh, and two doctors from the Harvard School of Public Health have written that "there is reason to suspect that the effects will include increases in cancer, heart disease, stroke, and blindness." But that's all.

To determine whether health-conscious snackers will mind suffering strokes, blindness, and ass swamp, Frito-Lay Inc., the manufacturer of the first olestra-fortified snacks, is test-marketing its revolutionary chips in only three cities: Cedar Rapids, Iowa; Grand Junction, Colorado; and Eau Claire, Wisconsin. But, because I'm a powerful editor at the fifth-best paper in town, I managed to score some samples of Frito-Lay's new line of olestra-laced Max chips.

Last week, I called Frito-Lay world headquarters in Plano, Texas, and said, "Hey, I work for *The Met*. Can I get me some of them space-age fat-free chips?" After I explained what *The Met* was, a Frito-Lay Snack Official told me I could drive out there and pick some up. So I did. (A note about Frito-Lay world headquarters: Remember in *Conan the Destroyer* when Arnold Schwarzenegger, Grace Jones, and Wilt Chamberlain sneak into Castle Grayskull or wherever to rescue the virgin princess? Well, Frito-Lay headquarters is like Castle Grayskull, insofar as it's *way* bigger than my house.)

I got three samples: a yellow bag of Original Lay's Max, a blue bag of Ruffles Max, and a red bag of Nacho Cheesier Doritos Max. I took them back to the office for a taste test and a loose-stool experiment.

(Note about the testing procedure: My test was like the new Keanu Reeves action flick, *Chain Reaction*, insofar as it involved a lot of bad science. Specifically, my experiment had neither a control group nor a test group large enough to draw any valid conclusions.)

When I told everyone that I had the new fat-free chips not yet available in area stores and that I needed to enlist their help as snack researchers, several co-workers knocked me to the floor and wrestled the bags from my arms. They unanimously agreed that the Frito-Lay's Max potato chips are a snackalicious marvel of modern food technology. The chips offered the same crisp crunch, great taste, and velvety mouth feel as the fatty versions of Ruffles, Lay's, and Doritos.

The female researchers, in particular, seemed to enjoy the salty snacks lubricated with the miracle olestra molecule. When I pointed out the labels warning of possible abdominal cramping and loose stools, one woman said, "Cramps? I already have 'em. Loose stools? Who cares? These are the best things ever." She would not relinquish her bag of Ruffles.

Myself, I ate about three or four servings of each chip flavor, considerably more than the recommended dosage. Then I sat at my desk, feeling like I'd just eaten a handful of psychedelic mushrooms, afraid of what might happen but growing impatient that nothing was. Later that night, My Fair Lady threatened to kick me out of the house, so voluminous and rotten were my nether zephyrs. But that was it. In terms of actual stools, I had no technical difficulties.

Until the next day. The next day, something went awry in my alimentary canal. Terribly awry. Over the course of one hour, I visited the lavatory no fewer than three times. Each visit produced much gurgling and splashing. I don't wish to offend and so will sum it up with one word: "schlitterbahn."

All in all, though, I have to agree with my female colleagues. Loose stools? Who cares? Now I can snack like John Candy without growing so enormous that I'll have to purchase two tickets when I fly coach. See you in the john.

Editor's note: Who knew that John Candy would go and die and make that last joke seem so insensitive? And that Frito-Lay would rename its line of olestra chips Wow!?

A Sanitized-by-Swisher Facility
Is Clean, Pleasantly Fragrant,
and Safe for Everyone

SEVERAL EVENINGS PAST, WHILE RELIEVING MYSELF AT AN AREA tavern's urinal, I looked down and was puzzled by what I saw. No, not that. I've grown used to that over the years. What nonplussed me was the Swisher-brand red plastic sieve onto which I was urinating. Specifically, these words, which appeared on it:

"SAY NO TO DRUGS."

What, I wondered, would Marshall McLuhan have to say about this message and its micturitional medium? I mean, let's say I were considering taking up crystal meth. I've got some crystal-meth-snorting strippers I hang out with, and they've extended an invitation to get hopped up like ferrets in estrus and take naughty pictures of each other covered in condiments and FTP them to the Internet. Do the folks at Swisher really hope, even for a second, that I'll look down at their urinal sieve — the one I'm currently pissing on, with the wodge of gum on it and also two soaked Camel butts — and go, "Wait a sec. Crystal meth is bad. I'm going to SAY NO TO DRUGS"? Because if that's the case, the urinal sieve's message ain't gonna get through. Point your browser to www.highonmeth.com/rogers_assrelish.

Well, as luck would have it, Swisher also prints a toll-free 800 number on its urinal sieves, so I called to get some answers. The number got me to Swisher International headquarters in North Carolina, but an operator told me I needed to speak to my local office and transferred me accordingly. At length, I reached Randy Dixon, a franchise owner here in Dallas. Randy sounded like a swell, but busy, fellow. I got right to the point.

"I'm not sure what the technical term for them is, but I have a question about your urinal sieves."

"The insider's technical term is 'screen,' " Randy said.

"Excellent. Screens. So I was in a bar recently, Randy, peeing on one of your fine urinal screens."

"Good. We appreciate that."

"Don't mention it. And I noticed that the screens have a message printed on them: SAY NO TO DRUGS."

"Correct," Randy said.

"I'm not trying to diminish the importance of urinal screens.

Don't get me wrong. But of all the things you could put a message on ... I mean, it's still something you piss on."

"Right."

"And you're basically trying to get someone to change his life."

"Yeah, you know, I just don't know who's responsible for that. It's been on there for years. I was in a meeting one time, and some people asked, 'Why don't we change that?' But nobody could come up with anything better, so I guess they just kept it. I really don't know."

Randy suggested I call corporate headquarters but said he didn't know who handled urinal-screen propaganda. He guessed purchasing. So I got back on the horn to headquarters and was subjected to many minutes of hold time, during which a golden-throated Swisher pitchman told me, "A sanitized-by-Swisher facility is clean, pleasantly fragrant, and safe for everyone," and, "Swisher International: dedicated to your satisfaction."

At length, I reached Barbara Coffee, who, though she may have been clean, pleasantly fragrant, and safe for everyone, was definitely not dedicated to my satisfaction. Barbara said she didn't know where the message came from, and when I asked if there was someone else who might, she said, "I don't know. I really don't. I'm sorry I can't help you." I practically had to threaten her with kung fu, but Barbara finally put me through to Amy Simpson, the company's vice president of operations. She had my answer — sort of.

According to Amy, Swisher's president, one Patrick Swisher, put the message on his urinal screens back in 1983, because it was "popular." Amy said that in her seven years with Swisher, she's received only one complaint about the message, from a man who said it wasn't Swisher's business to tell him to say no to drugs. But as for my McLuhanary concerns, Amy didn't see anything odd about tackling weighty issues with a urinal screen.

So you can see my dilemma, right? Because I believe in the message. I endorse it. People should SAY NO TO DRUGS. You don't want to see my relish-slavered ass on the Internet, and neither does my wife. But no way can the message be taken seriously with everyone urinating on it.

So here's my solution, one I suggest you join me in: Whenever I find myself in a sanitized-by-Swisher facility, I now rescue the urinal screens from their ignominious lot. I dig them out with a pencil or somesuch and put them on the sink counter, where people can read the message and respect it. If I save one life, it will have been worth it.

Gretchen Mol Has Enormous Nipples

I CAN TELL YOU THIS: POURING HOT CANDLE WAX ON YOUR NIPPLES might *sound* like a good idea, but it's not. At all. Unless you've got really tough nipples. Which, it turns out, I don't.

Gretchen Mol led me to this discovery. Gretchen, in case you didn't know, is Hollywood's next "it" girl, according to the September *Vanity Fair*. Actually, the cover asks a question — "Is she Hollywood's next 'it' girl?" — but the article basically says yes, the tagging of Gretchen is imminent, at which point she will definitely be "it." To support this theory, the piece points to her upcoming roles in the Matt Damon vehicle *Rounders* and Woody Allen's *Celebrity*, also starring the lissome Leonardo DiCaprio.

Now, normally I don't read *VF*, my diet of periodicals consisting mostly of hard-core Filipino midget pornography and *Architectural Digest*, but I picked up the Gretchen Mol issue when I overheard two guys talking about it at Borders.

"Sweet Christ," one said to the other. "Would you look at these?"

"Someone call Customs. We've got ourselves a raisin smuggler."

Indeed. In the cover photograph, taken by Annie Leibovitz, Gretchen sports an Alberta Ferretti dress that's about as substantial as moist, off-brand, one-ply toilet tissue. And Annie must keep the thermostat in her studio turned *way* down, because Gretchen's nipples threaten to tear right through that Alberta Ferretti. We're talking preternaturally hard nipples. Attack nipples. Nipples that Gretchen could probably use to dial a rotary phone. Nipples that Gretchen could steer her car with when she's searching for toll change — in the back seat.

Based solely on the strength of Gretchen's nipples, I bought a *VF* and read the article with hopes of learning more about them. I was crestfallen to learn that her breasts were referred to only once and that nary a mention was made of her nipples proper (though the author, apparently possessed of a keen eye for all non-nipple-related detail, did devote several paragraphs to Gretchen's pet rabbit, which reportedly roams freely in her New York apartment).

After turning to my most recent issue of *Pygmy Poon* to relieve my disappointment with *VF*'s reporting, I got to thinking about the broader issue of nipples. They're mesmerizing, nipples are, in the literal sense. They have the power to boost magazine circulation. I do not doubt that a handsome set of nipples, sufficiently hardened and lovingly photographed by Annie Leibovitz, could launch a thousand ships.

But only if men were at the helms and the ship-launching nipples belonged to a woman. Right? I mean, I've never heard a woman say that she found a man's erect nipples attractive. No, women only get excited about silly, inconsequential stuff, such as a man's "personality" and his "willingness to validate her feelings and share in the upbringing of their child." So here we men are, equipped with these useless protuberances that will yield us neither milk nor magazine covers.

Thinking thusly, I was filled with rage. I shook a fist at the heavens and cursed the gods for outfitting me with worthless nipples. It was then that I understood my neurosis, what had driven me to buy that *Vanity Fair*: Yes, I have nipple envy.

I knew what I had to do. A few telephone calls convinced me that no one in town sells strap-on nipples. After trying in vain to MacGyver a mini-marshmallow-and-thread apparatus, I hit upon the idea of hot wax.

That's how I came to appreciate the tenderness of my nipples. Not right away, though. At first — I'm a little ashamed to admit — I sort of got turned on. I started to worry that I might be a closet masochist. You know? I just kept dripping more and more hot wax on my nipples, and I guess I got carried away, because before I knew it, I had Megazord-size nipples. Like, if Gretchen and I were to hug, we wouldn't be able to get our arms around each other.

The pain kicked in after the adrenaline wore off. But by then I'd put on a tight Hanes undershirt and gone to the mall to flaunt my newly augmented nipples. With every step through NorthPark, the Hanes rubbed my nipples, tugged at them, until my nipples felt as if they were on fire. I had to walk slouched over and with my shoulders thrust forward to keep the sandpaper Hanes off my poor, raw nipples. All of which was mild discomfort compared to the Chinese-torture-level pain that awaited me when I pretended to try on a pair of Levi's at JC Penney and ducked into a changing stall to peel *off* the wax and, in the process, removed a considerable number of areola hairs and skin, too. Not a pretty sight.

So I'll stay tuned to see if Gretchen Mol can parlay her nipples into an Oscar. But until I can fit into that Alberta Ferretti, I'm leaving my own peepers be.

Religion

I Was Distracted by the Hot Baptist Babes

A s I WALKED OUT THE DOOR LAST MONDAY EVENING WITH A BIBLE in one hand and a bottle of Old Weller 107 in the other, My Fair Lady looked at me sideways and said, "Where are you going?"

"I'm headed to a singles' Bible-study meeting. And I'll need to take off my wedding band, but I promise I'll remain faithful," I said. I added, "It's for Jesus, honey."

A friend of mine had told me about the Prestonwood Baptist Church Monday-night singles' Bible study. It's called "Metro," and reportedly about 2,000 singles turn out to praise Jesus and bone up on their scripture. That's a lot of singles.

I figured 2,000 Christians trying to make a love connection against the backdrop of their savior's death was a spectacle I shouldn't miss. The bourbon I brought along because I thought smelling like high-proof booze in a church full of Baptists would be a real hoot. You know, like someone would say, "Sir, have you been drinking?" And I'd say, "You're damn tootin', neighbor. And right before I came in, I did some dancing in the parking lot. I saw *Footloose*."

So it came to pass that I arrived at the Prestonwood Baptist Church, had a healthy pull on the Weller 107 before getting out of my car, and entered the sanctuary. Believe me when I tell you: The Prestonwood Baptists have one hell of an installation out there in North Dallas. Forget the Branch Davidians; the Prestonwood Baptists have a real compound. I'm guessing you could fit six or seven Death Stars inside the place.

In the lobby, I found the single Baptists — although I suppose there could have been a few Methodists and an Episcopalian or two, and some might have been married. The Prestonwood officials didn't seem to be checking papers. I'm Catholic, and I had my wedding ring tucked in the overlooked fifth pocket of my Levi's, yet I passed easily among them.

People milled about, clutching their Bibles, some of which were protected by special leather carrying cases — sort of like how you'd take care of a good pool cue or a bowling ball. The women, for the most part, appeared to me a little overdressed for Bible study: big hair, large quantities of makeup, equally large portions of perfume, and tight, sleeveless sweaters. The ladies seemed focused on the "singles" part of the singles' Bible study. The men did, too.

I adjourned to the sanctuary proper and found a red-cushioned pew toward the back. An enormous black banner, a curtain really, hung behind the altar/stage. Emblazoned on the banner in gold letters, and lit by a spotlight, was the word "MEtRO," with a lower-case crucifix "t." Energy rays emanated therefrom. I felt like an extra in a Leni Riefenstahl propaganda flick.

Shortly, the proceedings got under way. A five-piece band — complete with four backup singers, two guitars, a full drum kit, and a grand piano — took the stage and launched into a powerful contemporary Christian number. Everyone began clapping and stood to sing: "Jesus is a mighty warrior / dressed in armor of light. / He crushes the deeds of darkness / which is really right." Or words to that effect.

I watched one guy in the congregation, as he sang, extend both arms, palms facing the Metro banner as if he were pretending to be Iron Man and shoot plasma from his hands. I tapped a pen on the pew in front of me. That's about as far into it as I could get.

The band handed it over to Tommy Nelson, a strapping guy in charcoal Dockers who spoke in a deep, commanding drawl. Tommy had us turn to John 7:40 for the night's lesson. The people seated next to me found the passage immediately, but I fumbled with my Bible for some time before I remembered that John is part of the New Testament and therefore toward the back, not up in the Pentateuch, where I was looking. Plus, I'd never used my Bible before, so all its pages stuck together.

Tommy actually delivered a nice bit of speechifying on John 7:40-52. The point of the passage, if I understood it, was that you can't follow Christ with all your heart and be concerned with earthly matters: wealth and public stature and such. God doesn't want fence-sitters, I think Tommy said.

To be honest, I didn't follow along all that closely, on account of I was distracted by the hot Baptist babes, and I had taken that shot of Weller 107 on an empty stomach, so I felt woozy. But I was struck by one thing Tommy said. I took these words with me and will remember them always: "If you drink out of a stream, and a half-mile upriver beavers have been doing what beavers do, you'll puke like a buzzard."

Even an atheist would have to agree.

Enough With the Kisses!

I DO NOT HAVE A DAUGHTER. APPARENTLY THEY ARE GREAT THINGS TO have, these daughters. My friend has one, and he seems pretty attached to it. He'll often leave a bar way before everyone else is ready just because he has to pick it up at daycare or whatever.

I mention my not having a daughter because maybe that's the reason I don't get this "Butterfly Kisses" business. Have you heard this song? Bob Carlisle, who's a real clean-living Christian sort of fellow, always giving props to God et cetera, wrote "Butterfly Kisses" as a present for his daughter on her 16th birthday. I guess a car would have been too materialistic for good old Christian Bob. Bob's all about giving gifts from the heart.

But so "Butterfly Kisses" has, in Bob's words, "taken off like brush fire." The Butterfly Kisses album recently made it to No. 1 on the Billboard chart. When Oprah had Bob on her show on Father's Day to sing the song, there wasn't a dry nose in the house. Everybody who comes within a 5-mile radius of this powerful song breaks down in tears.

The chorus goes like this: "Butterfly kisses after bedtime prayer. / Stickin' little white flowers all up in her hair. / Walk beside the pony, Daddy, it's my first ride. / I know the cake looks funny, Daddy, but I sure tried. / Oh, with all that I've done wrong, / I must have done something right / To deserve a hug every morning / And butterfly kisses at night."

I don't know whether it's all the prayerful bedside action or Bob's crooning about how much he just loooves his precious little daughter, but this song makes me want lure my neighbor's dog into my house with a juicy steak and secure his four paws to my living-room floor with a nail gun so that his yowling cries might drown it out. I am not kidding. If you are my neighbor and you are reading this, keep an eye on Charlie.

And I'm not even going to bring up the whole matter of this song's talking about a guy stickin' stuff all up in his daughter's hair, much less the horse-riding imagery. Let's just say that it wouldn't surprise me if old Bob was once a Catholic priest.

Like I said, though, I don't have a daughter. I might be missing something. So I visited the Bob Carlisle Web site to investigate.

Bob's at bobcarlisle.com, where you can order all sorts of "Butterfly Kisses" paraphernalia. My favorite part of the Bob Carlisle site was the Butterfly Kisses Forum, where you can post messages about "Butterfly Kisses." There are hundreds of messages, and the thing I noticed was that every single one of them, without exception, positively gushed about how beautiful this song is.

"God sent our daughter to us through adoption," read one, "and she was halfway around the world in China!! She's absolutely Daddy's girl, and this beautiful, God-inspired song helps my husband remember how important he is to her life. Thanks, Bob!"

One in every five people on this planet is of Chinese descent. With those odds, I don't buy that God sent this couple their little China girl.

"I heard this song on the way into the parking lot at work today," read another. "I had to sit in my car and stop crying before I could come into the office. My husband and I have two little girls, and it sure hits home! I want to run home, hold tight to them, and not let go. I am still all choked up! What a beautiful gift you have given to all of the world with this song."

You know, so I was just itching to piss off these butterfly kissers, to stir up a little righteous Christian bile. I posted this: "Not to sound insensitive, but whenever 'Butterfly Kisses' comes on the radio, it reminds me that in certain countries, such as China, fathers still give the old 'burlap sack in the river' treatment to newborn daughters because they're not as strong as boys and therefore not as helpful around the farm et cetera. And I profoundly hate the song."

I figured I'd get flamed for weeks. But I got nary a response. Oh, boy, did that get my hackles up. So I posted: " 'Butterfly Kisses' is so sickly saccharine that I have to brush my teeth every time I hear it. Please make it stop! Enough with the kisses! Nine out of 10 dentists have declared Bob Carlisle public enemy No. 1. I pray to Jesus that he falls into a large vat of fluoride and is unable to visit upon us his mind-numbing, tooth-decaying rot. Long live Marilyn Manson!"

I checked back at the Butterfly Kisses Forum a few hours later and saw a response. It said: "I pray that you are kidding. If not, I pray for you to be blessed by God with the beauty and love of a child some day. But most of all, I pray that you will find an opening in your heart for Jesus. God bless you."

I'm getting my nail gun.

Real Men Love Jesus

Last Saturday morning, I was doing important research on the effects of long-term exposure to televised college football when my wife told me I ought to attend the Promise Keepers hootenanny that was under way at Texas Stadium.

She said, "You could use some Christ-centered ministry dedicated to uniting men through vital relationships to become godly influences in their world." Or words to that effect, adding, "Why don't you go stand in the gap?"

I was like, "Screw Christ. He and the rest of the Trinity and the Virgin Mary, too, are on my shitlist for allowing Notre Dame to have such a lousy record this year. You know how many Benjamins I lost on the USC game? Nonetheless, I bet two large on the Irish today, and I intend to lie right here and watch them trounce Boston College. Why would I want to fight traffic to sit in a stadium filled with 50,000 men crying and hugging each other — when there isn't even a game being played on the field?"

She pointed out that burning in hell hurts, so I made a strategic change of plans. I promised to attend. Truth be known, I had already arranged for press credentials in case Saturday turned out to be Judgment Day. I figured I could bust cheeks out to Texas Stadium in the early hours, during the light-to-moderate fire and brimstone. By the time the serious apocalyptic excreta hit the fan, I could blend in with the Promise Keepers, begging for mercy and lifting up my prostate or whatever.

Lucky for me, Saturday turned out to be just another Notre Dame Saturday, and I didn't hit a bit of traffic. I suspect this was due to the rally's beginning at 8:30 in the a.m. and my showing up at around noon. Just a guess.

Practically every other car I saw in the parking lot had stuck to its hind side one of those Christian fish or a bumper sticker that said something like "REAL MEN LOVE JESUS" or both. At the Gate 1 media check-in table, I was met by an alarmingly friendly Promise Keeper. He seemed secure in the knowledge that he was right with Jesus and therefore was not the least bit rattled by my *Red Meat* T-shirt, which depicted the shirtless torso of a man wielding a pistol, saying, "Not now, Honey. I'm on nude patrol."

The Promise Keeper's countenance seemed to say, very kindly and nonjudgmentally, "Have fun in hell, irreverent T-shirt boy." His mouth came right out and audibly said, "I was surprised to see that *The Met* was covering this event. Praise Jesus." (I might be making up the "praise Jesus" part.)

I said, "Yes, well. *The Met* isn't what you'd call a religious publication, for sure. But, lo, here I am to, um, conduct coverage."

And that is exactly what I did once I found a seat and a free Dr Pepper up in the press box. Here is what I saw, coverage-wise: phalanxes of folding chairs arrayed on the stadium floor, which was covered by a blue tarp; also on the stadium floor, a "Prayer Booth" that looked a lot more like a tent to me; a big, impressive stage, complete with faux, five-story Doric columns; groups of men wearing identical Day-Glo hats, some orange, some yellow, et cetera; groups of men wearing identical Day-Glo shirts; on a press-box monitor, Michigan playing Michigan State in a game of tackle football; entire stadium sections involved in a call-and-response that went, "We love Jesus. Yes we do. We love Jesus. How 'bout you?"; the wave; the seldom-seen double wave; and seven black people, give or take.

All of the above took place during what I learned was a lunch break. The onstage, postprandial proceedings that I covered went like this: Dennis Agajanian, who is the fastest Jesus-worshipping guitar strummer in the world (or something like that) and who looks like he wants to be Garth Brooks, got up and strummed his guitar real fast and generally let it be known that Jesus is Lord; lots of Day-Glo-outfitted white guys clapped their hands. That was all I could take. I saw some Promise Keepers personnel with suspicious 4-gallon buckets taking up position in the aisles, and I was afraid the press box wouldn't be exempt from making an offering, so I snuck out after only two hours of coverage and before I witnessed any actual speechifying.

I got home in time for the second quarter of the Notre Dame-Boston College game. I told my wife, "I said I would go, and I went. That makes me a promise keeper. Now I'm going to watch a stadium get used for its rightful purpose."

The Irish won 52-20. Praise Jesus.

Only God Knows for Sure WJWD

I F YOU'RE A GOOD CHRISTIAN, YOU'RE PROBABLY FAMILIAR WITH THE acronym WWJD. I'm not, so I had to ask.

"It's all the rage with the kids," a co-worker told me. "You got your WWJD shoelaces, your WWJD socks, your WWJD T-shirts. It stands for 'What Would Jesus Do?' "

"What would Jesus do?"

"Yeah, you know. It's supposed to be inspirational. Like you get in a jam and you look down at your shoelaces or whatever and you ask yourself, 'What would Jesus do?' My niece wears a bunch of multi-colored WWJD bracelets, probably five or six on each arm. I said to her, 'Those are cool. Can I have one?' She said, 'Sure. But it'll cost you.' "

"I don't think your niece grasps the concept," I said. "I'm guessing, first of all, that Jesus wouldn't wear 'What Would Jesus Do?' accessories. And if for some reason he were wearing 'What Would Jesus Do?' bracelets and you asked him for one, he'd probably give you the bracelets for free — all of them — and his sandals, too. Then he'd wash your feet with his hair or something."

But, in theory, this WWJD thing sounded like a good idea, so I headed out to the Bible Factory Outlet at Grapevine Mills to score a few. I hadn't done any Christmas shopping, and I thought WWJD bracelets would make great stocking stuffers. Giga Pets and WWJD stuff — that's Christmas magic!

The Bible Factory Outlet, in case you've never been, sells Bibles. They've got the *Super Giant Print Bible*, *The Inspirational Study Bible*, *The Women's Study Bible*, *The Mars and Venus Bible*, *The Choose Your Own Ending Bible* — all kinds. The Bible Factory Outlet also offers stuff like license plate frames that say, "Christians aren't perfect — just forgiven," and, "Warning: In case of Rapture, this car will be unmanned."

This latter one presents all sorts of religio-transit problems for me if that's how Rapture's going to work. I don't think they should let Christians be airplane pilots, for instance. Ditto for bus drivers.

And, of course, the Bible Factory Outlet sells the aforementioned WWJD bracelets. Also WWJD shoelaces. I bought three bracelets for $5.17, with tax. The funny thing about the actual purchase itself was that I accidentally cut to the front of a long line of shoppers because the bracelets were in an impulse grab barrel at the counter, and when I went up there to grab one, impulsively, the salesclerk just rang me up. You'd expect people shopping at a Bible Factory Outlet wouldn't mind cutting because of the whole "first shall be made last and last shall be made first" doctrine, but I didn't find that to be the case. When they glared at me, I asked myself, "What would Jesus do?" I wasn't prepared to give them all my earthly belongings and offer to die for their sins, so I just smiled politely and went on my way.

And that's the trouble. I've been wearing my WWJD bracelet now for almost a week. During that time, I've found myself in multiple situations where I've looked down at my bracelet, asked myself, "WWJD?" and either a) found myself unwilling to DWJWD or b) couldn't figure out WJWD.

Like when I was shopping for a Christmas tree and got really frustrated because I didn't want to spend an entire day's wage for some short-ass, needle-shedding fire hazard that I knew I'd just have to drag out to the curb in a few weeks. I looked down at my bracelet and asked, "WWJD?" And then I said, "No way am I ready to give all my money to charity and quit my job and wander from village to village, spreading the word of the Lord." In other words, "FWJWD."

Or, like just this morning, when I was putting the finishing touches on a grauwyler in the office lavatory and I realized, much to my chagrin, that there was no toilet paper in my stall. As I disconsolately held my forehead, I saw my bracelet and asked, "WWJD?" You know, I just couldn't answer that one. Maybe Jesus would call for divine intervention. Jesus was a well-known cheek turner. Maybe he knew a maneuver that would allow him to forgo the wipe altogether. Who's to say?

I've concluded that WWJD accessories might, in theory, make you a better Christian. In practice, though, they don't work nearly as well as good old Charmin.

Little Bopsy Wanted to Be a Fireman

MY FRIENDS SAY THEY'VE NOTICED A RECENT CHANGE IN ME. There's the new finishing move, of course. I've abandoned the Mandible Claw in favor of the Corporate Elbow, which has been working nicely. Smell what I'm cooking?

But that's not what they're talking about. My friends say that my heart has grown warmer. It's true, I tell them. And I owe it all to Heartwarmers4u.

A few weeks back, without my consent, a kind soul with Internet access put me on an inspirational e-mail list, Heartwarmers4u. A confirmation message came to me: "Your free e-mail subscription has been entered, and you will begin to automatically receive our inspirational and heartwarming stories, poems, and anecdotes."

I wondered how inspired I could possibly be by a organization that so wantonly split infinitives and that didn't pick up a dictionary to at least see whether "heartwarming" ought to perhaps — just maybe — be one word. My first inclination was to "surf" over to the Heartwarmers4u Web site and remove myself from its list, but perfecting the Corporate Elbow took longer than expected, and you better know your damn role. The messages started appearing the next morning.

The first one was titled "Thankful Thoughts #2" and led off with an ad for a mattress developed by NASA, yes, but it also included notes from other Heartwarmers4u members around the world describing what they were thankful for. One note from a woman in Virginia read: "I get down on my knees to thank God that I have legs to walk. ... I am drinking from my saucer because my cup overflows."

And I thought: I have legs. I more frequently use them to operate the clutch, gas, and brake pedals in my car, but just imagine all the places I *could* walk. I'm drinking from my saucer, too.

In the days that followed, I enjoyed stories about women who had ovarian tumors that vanished overnight as a result of prayer and men who could speak today only because God intervened on their behalves and stopped surgeons from cutting laryngeal nerves while they, the surgeons, were removing cancerous thyroid glands. As Heartwarmers4u suggested I might, I came to think of reading the messages that arrived every morning, relentlessly, as a "time-out oasis."

There was the story titled "Bopsy" about Bopsy, the little boy "dying of terminal leukemia," and Bopsy's mom. "Like any parent," the story went, "she wanted her son to grow up and fulfill all his dreams. Now that was no longer possible. The leukemia would see to that." Drat the evil leukemia!

The story had a bittersweet ending. Little Bopsy wanted to be a fireman, so the local fire station drove its ladder truck to Bopsy's hospital window, and the firemen climbed in to see him. "With his dying breath, Bopsy looked up at the fire chief and said, 'Chief, am I really a fireman now?' 'Bopsy, you are,' the chief said. With those words, Bopsy smiled and closed his eyes one last time."

Just like Heartwarmers4u said it would, that story really put things in the proper perspective. Because if there had been a fire that day, little Bopsy would have had a hard time fighting it, what with the leukemia and all.

But my favorite story so far has to be the very touching "Secret Ears." This one, too, concerned a boy with an affliction, though not terminal. He was born without ears. The other children tormented the earless boy, calling him "freak," according to the tale (the boy lacked only the external bits and could hear just fine).

The boy's father asked the doctor if anything could be done. "I believe I could graft on a pair of outer ears, if they could be procured," the doctor said. At the end of a two-year search, the father told his son, "Mother and I have someone who will donate the ears you need. But, it's a secret who it is." The operation went well, and the boy eventually married and entered the diplomatic service, without ever knowing the identity of the selfless, now earless, donor.

The story ended thusly: "The years kept their profound secret, but the day did come, one of the darkest days that ever pass through a son. He stood with his father over his mother's casket. Slowly, tenderly, the father stretched forth a hand and raised the thick, reddish-brown hair to reveal that the mother ... had no outer ears."

For me, the ellipsis there at the end really drove the point home. The story about the couple who found a rare and coveted Barney Banjo in a Pennsylvania Service Merchandise store with the assistance of a sales associate named Karen — a presumed Christmas angel, since the couple later learned that no one named Karen worked at that Service Merchandise and, what's more, the store had long ago sold out of Barney Banjos — that story was certainly touching. No question. But "Secret Ears" was something special. Truly ... heartwarming.

Notre Dame Is Not an Institution Interested in the Functionality of Condoms

THERE'S A GOOD CHANCE I DON'T LIKE YOU. LOOK AT IT THIS WAY: I have a small group of family and friends who watch the same limited number of TV programs I watch and who laugh at the same jokes I laugh at and who have the same skin color I have and who owe me money. These people I like.

Most of the rest of you, I don't like. You're dumb. You look nothing like me. Most of humanity, especially the Chinese, who make up one-fifth of the earth's population, fall into this group.

Then there are the people I truly hate. Admittedly, this is a small number of people. The chances of your being someone I truly hate are statistically slim but not insignificant. Because, trust me, if I truly hate you, you're on The List.

I keep The List. The List comprises names of people I truly hate. I cannot here name them all, for certain legal repercussions of defaming private citizens (even if they deserve to be truly hated). I can tell you that my List includes a dozen names. One of these names belongs to the kippy who slapped me, unprovoked, on the bus in the seventh grade.

Kippy, you know who you are.

Well, I was coping just fine and in an adult fashion with my true hatred, thank you, when a colleague mentioned how he'd recently added a fourth name to his own personal List. Whereupon I expressed profound amazement at his lack of hatred and his List's brevity.

"How can you possibly have only four people on your List?" I said. "You need to borrow a few?"

"Look," he said. "You're going about this List thing all wrong. You need to focus your hatred. Winnow your List to where you can send out negative energy to, say, five people, tops. My hatred is focused enough to mess up the people's lives on my List in a major way."

I got to thinking about my colleague's enlightened concept of hatred. He was right. Winnowing was in order.

Adele Lanan I shall name because she is the assistant director of student activities, media department, Notre Dame University, and therefore a public official. Adele held this position during my own matriculation at that fine institution. She enjoys the distinction of being the one and only person who has ever fired me.

At the time, I was a departments editor at *Scholastic*, the oldest continuously published student magazine in the country. To move the narrative along, Adele canned me, without warning, because I took particular pleasure in extolling the functionality of condoms within the pages of *Scholastic* and because Notre Dame was not, and is not, a institution interested in the functionality of condoms.

Well, so, I figured Adele was a prime candidate for pruning. Perhaps she had departed this earth or at least had gotten her karmic deserts. Then — *bang* — I'd be down to 11.

I called Adele and discovered that not only was she alive and kicking but she was on vacation. But Adele, God bless her, even though she was vacationing, returned my call. I could hardly contain my delight.

"You may not remember," I said, "but back in the day, I was a *Scholastic* staffer. Now I'm living in Dallas and I'm a columnist for a weekly magazine called *The Met* and I'm writing a column, um, well, tangentially about people who've affected me in my professional career. Uh, and whether you remember it or not, you were one of them."

"Ha, uh, ha-uh-huh," Adele laughed, good-naturedly, from, I imagined, Ixtapa.

"Because you *fired me!*" I said, also good-naturedly, from Dallas, not mentioning the several text books in which my writings have appeared, including *The Resourceful Reader* and *Motives for Writing*.

"Ahhh! I thought you rang a bell," she said.

"Eh, heh-heh-huh," I said. "The column I'm writing is actually about, uh, The List. The List, as I see it, is the List of people you will forever hate. Always and forever. Until either they die or something tragic befalls them."

"And so I'm on your List?" Adele asked, possibly from Chiang Mai.

"You've been on my List since '91," I said. "And, so, this column — actually I got into a conversation with a friend, and he convinced me my List is far too long. So I thought I would check in with you and first admit that I've, you know, done this terribly un-Christian thing and hated you since '91 and then, you know, find out if maybe you've lost a leg or if something horrible has happened to you and I can remove you from my List."

"I don't think I want to carry on this conversation," Adele said, solemnly, maybe from Yellowstone. "I'm very uncomfortable with it. So I think maybe you need to talk to somebody else."

"Okay. Well, uh. I understand."

"Okay."

"Thank you, Adele," I said.

You can see where I'm headed with this. The List stands at 12.

God Drank Beer Before Liquor
and Was Never Sicker

HERE'S A HYPOTHETICAL SITUATION FOR YOU: LET'S SAY YOU'VE worked hard all week. You've sweated your brow off to create something useful to humanity. You've left the world a better place than when you found it. What are you going to do at the end of that week?

Me, I'm going to blow off some steam. I'm going to get loaded like an Okie's pickup truck, start a fight with a guy bigger than me over whose quarters are up next on the pool table, and walk home from the bar because I can't remember where I parked my car.

The next day, I'll want to wake up late and leave sight of the television set only to find sustenance or eliminate waste — and then only if it's absolutely necessary. I've considered rigging myself with a colostomy bag to limit the number of times I have to get up off the living-room floor. Whenever I stop at the emergency room on my walk home, though, the medical technicians refuse to cooperate.

There exists a precedent for my case. On the seventh day, the Bible tells us, the Lord God ended his work which he had made. And he rested. For six days, he busted his hump creating night and day and the creatures that fly overhead and all the rest. On the seventh — though most interpretations from the original tongues overlook this detail — he watched television all day from his living-room floor.

The reason is obvious: God had a killer hangover. On the evening of the sixth day, when he saw that everything he had made was good, he went out and tied one on, and, since the universe was still young and such things weren't yet known, he mixed spirits, drinking beer before liquor. God was never sicker.

I have explained all this to My Fair Lady. I have even asked her to bring a Bible to my spot on the floor so I could prove, after you make the Jew-to-Christian conversion, that Sunday is the day for watching the Cowboys play the 49ers, especially considering the game's NFC playoff implications. But she won't listen.

"C'mon," she says, "you promised we'd buy new curtains for the bedroom this weekend."

"But the game," I say. "I gotta watch the game. I trust your taste. You buy the curtains."

She returns hours later with curtains that cost more than I would spend on my mother's casket, in addition to new curtain rods, which she insists are needed to complete the project, and several exotic potted plants. The plants are not needed for the curtain project. They are simply needed. And she is wearing the new shoes she bought. Also needed.

"Okay," she says. "Get your butt up. Time to hang curtains."

"The game," I protest.

"Those aren't the Cowboys and 49ers," she says. I've apparently been asleep for some time.

"Yeah, but the green team is in scoring position," I point out. "And, uh, it's gut-check time for the blue team. They have to make a defensive stand right here or ... um ... the green team will score. It's an important game." She is not impressed. "It's Sunday," I add.

But My Fair Lady favors a less literal interpretation of the Bible, so I have to get up and hang curtains instead of watch the green team and the blue team play what must be the biggest game of the year.

Well, last Sunday, I did something about my little Sabbath-breaking Jezebel. On Saturday, while we were out on the town, I secretly replaced the beer she usually drinks with Schlitz, brewed "with just the kiss of the hops." And I replaced it with a large volume of Schlitz, such that the hops wound up getting further with My Fair Lady than just a kiss.

As a measure of how much action the hops got that night, when we got back to the house, before she would come inside, My Fair Lady decided she had to run through the neighborhood, ducking from tree to hedgerow like she was playing S.W.A.T. Then she rang our doorbell, continuously, for five minutes.

My plan worked beautifully. The next morning, the Schlitz unleashed its full fury upon her. She crawled, bleary-eyed and gurgling, out of bed and into the living room, where she assembled a nest of blankets and pillows on the floor. She spent the remainder of the day waking at 30-minute intervals to see if she still had a headache or needed to go to the bathroom. All the while, projects went unfinished, much-needed accouterments remained on store shelves, and, with the floor occupied, I thanked God for the couch.

Sex

When It Came Time to Remove the Stitches, That Enviable Task Would Fall on Me or a Trusted Neighbor

I WAS THINKING ABOUT HAVING MY PENIS ENLARGED. NOT BECAUSE I'VE received any complaints or anything. (The customer is always right.) But I figured a few extra inches couldn't hurt.

Also, I saw a newspaper ad for the Men's Institute of Cosmetic Surgery. It offered me improved self-confidence through a one-hour surgery that could double my size. It said, "Dreams DO come true," and I could have "a 'NEW' life and be back to work the next day." (Joy! Joy!) The ad also said the surgery was impossible to explain over the phone (presumably for the same reasons the Church refuses to conduct my confessions via e-mail). As my good fortune would have it, though, the institute offered free 20-minute consultations, so I set up an appointment.

In the waiting room of the institute's North Dallas office, I filled out some paperwork and ate a few complimentary jelly beans before Jeff, my consultant, came out to greet me. Jeff was a young, clean-cut guy with a lot of starch in his shirt. He led me back to his office and took a seat at his desk. Behind Jeff hung framed medical certificates. They made me feel at ease. They were written in calligraphy, and to me, that just says "quality."

So Jeff began the presentation about making my penis bigger. Right away, I could tell why the explanation would have been impossible over the phone. A discussion of that sensitive nature required the use of visual aids. "We'll use this," Jeff said, producing a black Sharpie-brand marker, "to represent you."

Jeff explained that part of my marker is useless, because its cap lies behind my epidermal wall. Jeff explained that by cutting a suspensory ligament, Dr. Rosenstein could liberate that hidden portion, possibly giving me 3 added inches of prowess. (Self-confidence! Dreams coming true!) Jeff pushed the marker between his fingers to help me conceptualize this.

He also explained that the whole treatment, should I opt for it, would include taking fat cells from my belly and injecting them under the skin of my penis. This would give me the girth to match my new length.

Then Jeff wanted to know if I had any questions. "Yeah," I said. "This cutting of the suspensory ligament — is everything still going to be, you know, securely attached?" Jeff assured me that my marker would remain well anchored, but that I might expect to lose 10 degrees of what he referred to as "elevation." The Sharpie between his fingers drooped to reflect this.

"I've got some pictures," Jeff said, fear in his eyes, "if you want to see them." And before I knew it, I said yes and Jeff whipped out his photo album. It contained before and after pictures. All I can tell you about those, without getting arrested, is that "after" really means "within minutes after," like "before the iodine stains have been cleaned up." If Jeff gets pulled over by the cops and they find this photo album, he's going to get beat up.

Jeff wrapped up with the logistics. The procedures would together cost about $6,000. But that didn't include air fare to Los Angeles, where Dr. Rosenstein did the surgeries. And since I'd be back in Dallas when it came time to remove the stitches, that enviable task would fall on me or a trusted neighbor.

I left the institute relieved that the consultation didn't involve an actual inspection. Because when I met Jeff and we shook, his hands were cold. That, and he would have discovered that my penis doesn't look anything like a Sharpie marker.

My visit was great fun, but I've thought long and hard and decided not to have my penis enlarged. I think we men need to stick together on this penis issue. We need to stop putting so much emphasis on size and making each other feel self-conscious.

And don't blame the women for the pressure. Even though we men came up with Hooters, a restaurant that must make some small-breasted women feel inadequate, women haven't countered with a similar Poles restaurant, where plucky men wait tables in tight trousers.

So I'm not having the enlargement because I refuse to make my fellow man feel self-conscious. We should accept ourselves for who we are, darn it. Our dreams shouldn't be of larger penises. We should dream about happy families, loving relationships, and those business lunches at Hooters.

The Only Thing One Man Can Admire About Another Is Biceps

THE TROUBLE STARTED WHEN GIRL FRIENDLY'S ROOMMATE GOT herself a new beau. More precisely, the trouble started when I met him.

The four of us went out to one of those bars where they have small pool tables and serve vigorously marketed beer called Red Monkey or Red Beaver or whatever, and everyone wears cowboy boots, pretending they don't wear heels and penny loafers the rest of the week. You know the sort of place.

So we were just standing around, waiting for a turn on the pool table, drinking a Red Fish ("being our own fish," I think the slogan goes), when Girl Friendly turned to me and said, "I really like Dave." Dave was her roommate's new friend, so I didn't immediately have to beat him up. I knew Girl Friendly meant she *approved* of Dave. As in, "Dave is a sensitive man and seems to validate my roommate emotionally."

I wanted to seize the opportunity to agree with her, so I opened my mouth. That's when I said it. I don't know if it was the Red Pig talking or what, but what I said was totally unexpected. I don't think I've ever said anything like that about another man in my life. It just came out.

What I said was this: "Yeah, I like him, too. And he's *really* good-looking."

That's what I said. Not, "He's handsome," or, "I like the cut of his jib," or even just, "He's good-looking." I said he was *really* good-looking.

It's not that I'm afraid I have homosexual tendencies. I don't think I do, but it would be fine if I did. The way I look at it, as long as I could keep having heterosexual tendencies, which I guess would mean I would then have bisexual tendencies, having homosexual tendencies would just double the number of people I could ogle. Maybe Michael Stipe and I could do lunch.

No, what bothers me about saying Dave was really good-looking is that, of course, Girl Friendly passed the comment on her to roommate. "I really like Dave," her roommate later said. "Tim said he was '*really* good-looking,'" Girl Friendly offered.

And, naturally, her roommate told Dave what I said. So, basically,

I may as well have walked up to Dave in the bar and lispingly whispered in his ear that I wanted to take him over my knee and spank him for being a naughty boy.

Maybe I'm overreacting, but I don't think so. I know how guys think. From now on, whenever Dave sees me, even though I have a girlfriend and frequently demonstrate my heterosexuality by telling vulgar jokes and dressing poorly, he's going to think I want to spank him. And let me assure you, I've never even had the urge to reprimand Dave, much less spank him.

The whole incident has shown me that same-sex complimenting is unfair. Women can say whatever they want. I've heard one woman say about another, "She is so beautiful. Her hair looks lustrous and manageable." Nothing is out of bounds. Women routinely express their jealousy and will say things such as, "Her boobs are like rockets! God, I wish I had rocket boobs like hers."

Do you see what I mean? No self-respecting man, even if he thinks it, can say, "Chuck sure has tight buns. I wish I had tight buns like Chuck's." No sir. Not if you ever want to work with power tools again.

The only thing one man can admire about another is biceps. The biceps are safe. No glutes or quads. Occasionally, we can get away with an appropriately rugged-sounding comment about another man's abdominals, but it stops there. No hair compliments allowed.

And when we say something about biceps, it has to follow a strict protocol. For instance, it would not be proper procedure to say, "His arms look all big and strong." Absolutely not. We have to say, "He has guns." We must borrow terms from the field of weaponry to describe each other. And it is not acceptable for a guy to say he wants guns like another guy's. Just, "He has guns," or, "Damn, he has guns." That's it.

Something needs to be done about this. I predict we will never have true equality between the sexes until men feel free to tell each other when we look handsome and are having a good hair day. We need studies done on the subject. Maybe the Swedes have already resolved the issue and they can teach us how to handle it.

Until we straighten this out, though, I'm going to stay away from the Red Weasel and keep my mouth shut when I see a cute guy.

Then She Opened Her Special Place to Him

READ THE OTHER DAY THAT PEOPLE BUY ALMOST $1 BILLION WORTH OF romance novels a year, and the romance category accounts for nearly half of all mass-market paperback purchases. There's a woman, Jayne Ann Krentz, who writes under the name of Amanda Quick. Last year, she made the *New York Times* bestseller list with five different books. She's got 20 million books in print.

I've got to get a piece of this action. This Krentz woman was a librarian before she started writing romance novels. Imagine how successful a trained content provider like me could be.

So I conducted some research. I went out and bought a few paperbacks featuring swarthy, bare-chested men on their covers, and I read them. Judging from my sample group, "romance novel" is just another term for "smut" — but with a lot of plot getting in the way of the action. I can write smut.

This week, I'm going to treat you to an excerpt from my first romance novel. It will be titled *Dreams of Length and Width*, and my nom de plume will be Richard Cummings. I've spared you all the boring parts with the plot:

His lips were soft.

And hard.

And his tongue was like a concrete bit on the end of a variable-speed Black & Decker drill. It was unrelenting as it sought entrance, and she surrendered it gladly.

She wanted this Jake Broadfellow, this man who was not who he seemed, who was both gentle and rough.

God, how Chastity Flemming wanted him.

How she craved him. Oh, God.

Her body moved by itself ... closer to him ... and she knew without knowing it, knew it at the level of her cells that she wanted to feel his chest against her breasts. Closer. Closer. And then the contact. Shivery. Electric.

His manly chest hairs felt like a thousand tiny electric eels, only not slimy like eels. Like dry electric eels. And they worked their magic on her swelling breasts. His tongue danced with hers as his upper torso moved in combination with his lips, like some glorious taffy-pulling machine. Back and forth. Back and forth.

She raised her head and looked at Jake. His eyes were as the heating element on an electric stove, burning bright and hot.

"Oh, Jake," she said.

"Oh, what?" Jake said.

"Just oh, Jake," she said.

This tingling that started at the sweet friction of Jake's lips teasingly tasting hers had migrated through his ministrations to an area where, for her, only the backs of horses ever touched. Except one fence post. And the handle of the vacuum cleaner. But besides the fence post and vacuum cleaner, nothing but the backs of horses had ever touched her there.

Before Chastity knew what she was doing, she touched Jake and found a pulsating shaft of iron. She sucked in her breath at the thought of what God had wrought. Yes, God was quite a blacksmith to have crafted such a manroot as belonged to Jake Broadfellow.

Then she opened her special place to him, and he slid slowly inside, filling her. If you've ever seen a butcher filling a pig's intestine's with meat to make sausage, that's sort of what Jake was doing. Only much more tenderly. And roughly.

This was more than friendship. This was that other thing, that secret thing.

"Oh, Jake ... it's so beautiful."

"You are beautiful," Jake said. "This is love."

She rode over terrain she had only dreamt about, under an animal so wonderful that she experienced every fleshy inch of the way. The pleasures inside her body multiplied until they were one great bursting ecstasy of dreams indulged, fantasies fulfilled, imagination satisfied. Her mind spun into a space and time that were endless, and her eyes rolled back into her head like a crazed zombie. Sparks shot out of her tear ducts and explosions rippled through her body.

Jake made a grunting noise, and his whole body went stiff for a second. Then he abruptly rolled over and clicked on the television just in time to catch a rerun of an Australian rules football game on ESPN.

"Whew," Jake Broadfellow said. "That sure was good, baby."

The end.

Editor's note: Many thanks to Barbara Cummings for her inspirational book Fortune's Fire.

Martha Stewart Is the MacGyver of the Bedroom

YOU KNOW THAT GAME WHERE YOU SIT AROUND WITH YOUR FRIENDS and everyone names the celebrity he or she most wants to have sex with? Girls always pick Brad Pitt or Antonio Banderas. Guys go for Pamela Anderson Lee or Liv Tyler.

Me, I want to diddle Martha Stewart, the genteel dominatrix of domesticity. I'd like visit Martha's Turkey Hill farm in Westport, Connecticut, and have her give me a private tour of her henhouse. I'd like to romp through her garden and give her buttermilk a vigorous alfresco whisking. An outdoor setting, as you know, implies informality in dress and menu, so Martha could wear her khakis while she trimmed my rhubarb. Her cat Teeny could watch.

In my opinion, there could be no better screw than Martha Stewart. Forget the Kamasutra. Martha has probably *forgotten* more secret lovemaking techniques than the Hindus will ever discover. She's the MacGyver of the bedroom. Got some mismatched flatware you no longer use? With her handy smelting furnace and a small electrical motor, Martha could mold the flatware into a stainless-steel vibrating dildo.

My Martha Stewart fantasy only grew when *Time* magazine named her one of America's 25 most influential people. Cutting-edge housekeeping skills *and* influence? Bestill my beating loins.

I have no delusions, though. If I were one day to meet the lovely Martha — say, if I crashed the *Today* set and professed my yearning for her on live national television — she probably would not bid me to partake of her bounteous spread.

So I resolved to make myself worthy. I decided to learn and follow just one of Martha's domestic tips. I would pick the simplest chore, one I could complete successfully. The act itself, I thought, would bring me closer to Martha, the divine Homemaker.

I went out and bought the current issue of Martha's magazine, *Martha Stewart Living*. I eagerly read about many household projects. I read about painting floors ("... try to remember that the same rules apply to painting a floor as to the rest of life. Be prepared. Don't expect perfection. And always leave yourself a way out"). I read about planting ground cover ("if pittosporum, yew, and photinia have become front-yard clichés, the big three ground covers at their feet look just as predictable and trite"). But everything seemed hopelessly beyond my means and ability — until I read about how to make serving bowls of ice. Oh, joy!

Basically, the process involved getting two glass or stainless-steel containers of differing sizes, suspending the smaller inside the larger with masking tape, filling the space between with water (and edible flowers, fresh herbs, or citrus slices), and, finally, freezing the water. Surely, I could handle this.

When I arrived home with the magazine, I expected questions from My Fair Lady. "What are you doing with that magazine? Do you think Martha Stewart has a cuter butt than I do?" Stuff like that.

Instead, she said, "Oh, I'm so glad you brought that home. There's a great tip in that issue that I wanted to save."

"What tip?" I asked.

"It's all about how to make these cute serving bowls out of ice!"

I am not making this up. My Fair Lady had bought *Martha Stewart Living*, read about the innovative ice bowls, and misplaced her copy. She was very excited about my attempt to fashion the ice bowls (not knowing, of course, that I was doing it to get in Martha's pants).

I banged around in the kitchen but couldn't find any stainless-steel or glass bowls of differing sizes, so I was forced to use two plastic cups. This, I knew, was not how Martha would do it. I also had no edible flowers handy, so for decoration I had to improvise with raw spaghetti and chopped bay leaves. I taped up the whole apparatus, filled its crevice with tap water, and stuck it in the freezer.

The next morning, I was so excited that I almost peed in my jammies. I opened the freezer, and, lo, I did have a glass made of ice. But the spaghetti had kind of dissolved, making the ice all yellow. Plus the bay leaves looked like dirt.

When I offered my ice sculpture for My Fair Lady's appraisal, she said, "Grody. That doesn't look anything like Martha Stewart's."

My Fair Lady and I had sex later that night, despite my failure. It was beautiful, transcendent. I couldn't help but think, though, *Is this how Martha would do it?*

My Eyes Did Not Wander From the Handsome Cut of Meat on My Plate

I T WOULD BE AN UNDERSTATEMENT TO SAY THAT MY FAIR LADY WAS not overjoyed to learn I had plans to eat dinner at a topless club. Her main problem with topless clubs, as I understand it, is that they oftentimes feature bare breasts — specifically, *other women's* bare breasts. No sir, MFL is not big on the idea of my looking at other women's breasts.

I once took her to a topless joint so she could see for herself what goes on in such places. She comes from back East, where topless clubs aren't the cultural institution they are here in Dallas, so she'd never before seen the inside of one. I don't think, after her inaugural experience, she'll be going back anytime soon.

Her comments to me ran pretty much along these lines: "That stripper is only wearing chaps!"

To which I responded, "Honey, the chaps protect her legs from bull nettle and various other nasty weeds that grow out on the range. Also, she probably prefers that you refer to her as a 'dancer' or 'entertainer.' "

She said, "These beers are expensive!"

I responded, "Tap the Rockies."

"You were looking at her breasts!"

"Was not!"

"Were, too!"

"Was not!"

"He's staring at her uterus!"

This observation she made while watching an entertainer crab-walk down two handrails, her outspread legs forming an angle approaching 180 degrees. A guest stood at the bottom of the stairs. He held a $5 bill folded lengthwise. He had a glazed look in his eyes, what soldiers call the 1,000-yard stare, and he had it focused on the vertex of the woman's obtuse angle.

I said to MFL, "The gentleman obviously wishes to show the young lady how much he appreciates her dexterity and hard work. Plus, you're exaggerating slightly, my sweet. Texas has very strict regulations that prohibit the viewing of uteri in topless establishments."

All to no avail. My Fair Lady had seen enough and was ready to leave before we even finished our complimentary popcorn. She pronounced all topless bars "disgusting."

So she was not pleased when I told her about dinner at The Lodge, an upscale gentlemen's club. In a strictly professional capacity, I had participated in a Lodge-organized fishing tournament at Lake Fork, and while the tournament itself produced far more bass than breasts (in my boat, there was a 5:0 ratio of fish to tits), the club's owners scheduled an après-fish celebratory dinner at The Lodge. There, breasts would be present.

"The chicks will shake their junk in your face," MFL said.

"No they won't," I said. "The Lodge isn't like that other place I took you to. It's, like, classy ... and stuff."

She wasn't impressed.

"It has a taxidermied bear in the lobby," I said.

Nothing.

"I promise, if the chicks shake their junk in my face, I won't look at it."

With that assurance, she let me eat dinner at The Lodge, which I can say, with total objectivity, was a fabulous meal. That I did not have to pay for it should not concern you. The prime rib, served with a playful yet not overpowering horseradish, was so tender that it almost chewed itself.

My two dining companions and I, along with the rest of the fishermen from the tournament, ate in The Lodge's homey "Library," where books and more taxidermied critters lined the walls, watching us eat from above. The music was quiet enough to allow easy conversation. The service was impeccable.

Even when my friend's loaded baked potato unexpectedly leapt from the table and exploded on impact with the floor, sending bacon slivers and chives everywhere, management did not ask us to leave. A gracious waitress had the mess cleaned up directly.

As for the entertainment, I'm afraid I have nothing to report. I am told by my dining companions that it was excellent, but as I did not allow my eyes to wander from the handsome cut of meat on my plate, I can neither confirm nor deny this. When our plates were cleared, I stared at my spoon.

The only thing I can tell you is that world leaders, including members of the United Nations, sometimes eat at The Lodge, because one of my friends said he saw Boutros Boutros-Ghali.

Strippers Are Not to Be Trifled With

YOU KNOW HOW WHEN YOU WERE YOUNGER AND YOU LIVED WITH your parent(s), like when you were 23, and you didn't understand why you couldn't stay out till 5 a.m. and come home smelling like peppermint schnapps, with one shoe missing and your dilated pupils the size of nickels? Remember? And your parent(s), after arguing with you until your buzz was only a fond, distant memory, finally just said that you couldn't stay out till 5 a.m. and come home smelling like peppermint schnapps et cetera "because I (we) say so, and as long as you live under my (our) roof, you'll do as I (we) say"?

Yeah, well, unless you're my wife, you don't live with me. I can't influence your behavior by threatening to force you into an unpleasant, roofless life. So I'm going to explain, exactly, in easy-to-follow terms and in detail, why you can't — or shouldn't — date strippers. (And if you're my wife and you're interested in dating strippers, then that's a matter best handled someplace else besides this column, on a one-on-one basis. Or maybe two-on-one. But let's discuss.)

Over the years, I have had several friends date strippers (exotic dancers, whatever). I mention this to establish my credibility in the field of stripper dating and also to allay the ire of the strippers who have dated my friends and who might be reading this. Ladies, this column is not about you. Or at least it's not *solely* about you. So if you're reading this and thinking about pouring sugar in my gas tank or something, just put on some White Snake and relax. All the unflattering details are based on my *other* friend who dated that *other* crazy-ass stripper.

Here, then, is "The Story of Cautionary Tail: What Happens When You Date a Stripper": My friend — I'll call him Lichard — shows up to the gym one day so flagrantly happy that he looks like he might hug me, even though I'm sweaty and smell totally not huggable. I haven't seen Lichard at the gym in four months, so I know something's up. And before I can even ask Lichard what's up, he says, "Dude, so last night, I met this stripper, a friend of a friend, and before I know it, we're in my Jeep and she's telling me what a turn-on it is for her to drive around topless and how horny she is and turn right because she loves to cruise Greenville topless and did I mention she's a stripper? No tan lines."

This is Stage 1. Lichard, whose most noteworthy sexual exploit heretofore was receiving a handjob on the lawn at Starplex during a concert by the Church in 1988 and whose health regimen entails basically smoking filtered cigarettes and carrying around his gym membership card in his wallet, has gotten his first taste, so to speak, of stripper. He is hopped up. Ready to pump iron. Get fit. New lease on life. The world is his oyster. Et cetera.

About three weeks later, I meet Lichard after work for a few cocktails. There are signs that all is not right in the land of silicone and G-strings. While regaling me with stories of after-hours orgies, involving all manner of over-the-counter and prescription pharmaceuticals, Lichard is interrupted by a page.

"Dude," he says, fiddling with the thing clipped to his belt, "she never stops. She's a party animal. It's out of control."

This is Stage 2. Lichard, who required a solid week of recuperation after that alfresco handjob in 1988, is being asked to perform at a level to which he's unaccustomed. He is afraid. Riddled with performance anxiety. Sleep deprived.

A few weeks following that, I get a call from Lichard. He is in hiding. He refuses to disclose his location because I'm on a portable phone, and he's afraid the stripper might be monitoring our conversation. He wants advice.

"Tell me how to shake her," Lichard pleads. "I've tried everything. She won't leave me alone. She shows up at my office and wants to have sex on my desk. I told her I was gay. She just got hornier. The drugs, the sex, the topless driving — how do I end it? Make it stop!"

This is Stage 3. Lichard has come to realize that strippers are not to be trifled with. They are, in essence, professional, highly trained party people. Neither rain, nor sleet, nor lack of sleep will keep them from their appointed orgies and speedballs and all-night rumpusing.

Listen, strippers take drugs you've never even heard of. Strippers make more money than you do. Strippers are younger than you are. Strippers get up at noon and start looking for trouble; you need a nap by noon. So take my advice: Put the stripper down. Step away from the stripper. Nobody needs to get hurt here.

In Case You Are Wondering, Martina Hingis Swallows

WITH MY FAIR LADY OUT OF TOWN, OSTENSIBLY FOR BUSINESS reasons, I set about securing some high-grade porn. Not because I have the runaway libido of a chimpanzee and am unable to go without gratification for even a few days. More because: Why not?

As those of you in the industry know, the hottest trend in erotica today is hypnography. Amateur video porn? That's, like, so 1996. The real action is on audio CD. Guided imagery. Mild hypnosis. Aural smut. As in "Do not use this CD while driving or using heavy machinery."

So read the warning label on *Hypnography for Men*, the disc I had had the foresight to phone-order from a place in Hoboken, New Jersey, several days prior to My Fair Lady's departure. Normally, I like to do a little lathe work in the garage while I enjoy my porn, but I believe in following instructions, so I listened to *Hypnography for Men* in the living room, alone, undistracted by machinery.

The disc began with a soothing, synthesized soundscape of flutes. Then came a woman's voice. She sounded Anglo. Accent free. Probably in her early 30s. Sexy, but not whorish. Not like those 900-number harlots who punctuate every sentence with an "ooohh-yeah-baby." She sounded like she did voice-overs for luxury motorcar commercials when she wasn't doing porn. She sounded as if she were accustomed to wearing expensive shoes. But whoever wrote her script deserved a good keelhauling.

She began by saying, "Lay down, with your feet apart and your arms at your side."

"Lay down?" I thought. "Poor grammar like that is not going to get the job done. I should have known better than to order smut from a place in Hoboken." I turned down the stereo a notch so that my downstairs neighbor wouldn't hear me listening to ungrammatical hypnographic porn.

But I followed instructions and lay naked, past participle up, down on the floor. The Anonymous Hobokener Narratrix continued on, leading me through a relaxation exercise. She told me to let my thighs droop loose and limp, to feel my eyelids growing heavier and smoother. I obeyed. I imagined all my tensions, all my tightness, all my fears and worries draining from the top of my head.

The trouble started at about eight minutes into it. I was floating, drifting more and more into relaxation, focusing my attention gently and lazily on the tip of my nose, when she said, "I want you to now imagine that I am releasing a drug into the air. ... Breathe in the gas, sending you deeper and deeper into hypnosis."

"Aargh! A split infinitive!" I gasped. "Not to mention the room is filling with gas!"

The Hobokener then brought me to the top of a staircase that led to a "safe and beautiful place." The staircase had 10 steps, and each one left me feeling even more relaxed. When we got to the safe and beautiful place, she informed me that I felt "fabulous and secure." She also told me to notice the bed, which was covered with velvet. And the large, oversize movie screen.

"This is like that guy's house in *Silence of the Lambs*," I thought. "It's a basement rec room where I can wear night-vision goggles and play dress-up and fashion myself a suit of human skin."

The Hobokener had me visualize on the movie screen the most sensual creature imaginable. I pictured 17-year-old tennis sensation Martina Hingis. And Martina came to life — only not really, because the Hobokener described her as "ghostlike." Before I knew what happened, Martina slipped me an "orgasm pill" that, I was informed, took control of my penis, making it grow and grow. It got stiff, erect, and hard. It grew larger, firmer, and stiffer.

"Now imagine the movie screen is a mirror," the Hobokener said. "Take notice of yourself on the bed. You are completely naked, and you are delighted in your appearance."

"No I'm not," I thought. "I'm doped up on gas and lying naked on a velvet bed in my rec room, which is haunted by the ghost of Martina Hingis. Worse yet, I've lost control of my penis!"

Well, I proceeded to perform cunnilingus on Martina's hingis as she floated above me. This made me even harder. My penis, in fact, looked like a branch on a tree. I feared that I might exceed the operational limits of my penis, in terms of rigidity, but Martina finally returned the favor. I was told it was the best oral sex I had ever experienced. (In case you are wondering, Martina swallows.)

I thanked Martina for her ministrations, and the Hobokener led me back to awareness and my living-room floor. "You are happy with the way you performed," she said. "Your performance was excellent, and you are proud of that."

"At least it's nice to be told so," I thought. Then I repaired to the garage to really get to work with my lathe.

Tommy Lee Honks the Boat Horn
With His Penis

LISTEN TO ME: DO NOT WASTE YOUR TIME ON THE PAMELA AND Tommy Lee video. I'm not kidding about this. For erotic entertainment, you'd do better watching that *Aeon Flux* cartoon on MTV, the one where the girl on steroids runs around in a leather thong, acrobatically shooting people in the eye.

If you're a goatherd and missed the news, here's a recap: Pamela, she formerly of *Baywatch*'s beach, and Tommy, he of Motley Crüe's drüms, made a home movie in 1995. Said tape — 40 minutes of boating, mostly, punctuated by a little X-rated rumpusing — was stolen from the Lees' hotel room. After two years of legal wrangling, a judge ruled that Seattle-based Internet Entertainment Group could legally sell the tape. It hit stores this month. And, at almost $40, it's a gyp.

I know, I know. You guys are saying, "But it's Pamela Lee. Naked. How bad can it be?" Bad. Way worse than *Barb Wire*. And when it comes to flesh, Tommy's shaky-cam technique wastes Pamela's talents.

You (filthy) girls are saying, "But I heard Tommy has a colossal pants Picard." Right. Fine. So does 7-foot-7 Rumanian roundballer Gheorghe Muresan, but you don't want to see his unit, either. Trust me. If it's sheer size you want, visit the zoo.

As a special reader service, I herewith present the highlights of the tape, so that you can spend your time and money more wisely (huffing spray paint, perhaps):

The video opens with Tommy interrupting an uncharacteristically demure Pamela as she bathes. The lighting is good, but Tommy's camerawork is shoddy.

"You must be really bored," Pamela says.

"That's a negative," Tommy says. "I look forward to watching this back — and spanking my monkey."

An awkward editing jump puts the camera in Pamela's equally unsteady hands, a predictable bit of turnabout. She zooms in on his crotch and says, "Get naked or something. Do something."

The Lees' casual attention to technical quality and cinéma vérité approach to video tempt one to allude to Jean Rouch and Edgar Morin's seminal 1961 film, *Chronique d'un Eté* ("chronicle of a summer"). But that would be a mistake.

After a brief scene from the Lees' alfresco wedding, in which

Pamela conspicuously chews gum, we find the couple on a private yacht cruise. Below deck, Tommy goes shirtless, revealing a pierced right nipple and multiple tattoos, including, in 200-point bold Gothic letters across his solar plexus, the word "MAYHEM."

Pamela videos her hand grabbing Tommy's crotch. He accommodates her by brandishing his flaccid unit at the camera.

Moments later, Tommy says, "You're the sexiest fucking girl on the planet. Baby, I love you." They kiss. Pamela says, "Where are we?" Then she says it again.

Later, Tommy gets naked topside and tucks his penis between his legs. Pamela comments, "Where are we?" She repeats this three times in a row. Tommy answers, "We're on a big-ass yacht. I lost my dick." "That's a catastrophe," she says.

Cut to the cabin of their sports-utility vehicle, apparently several days post yacht cruise, as the couple tows their own personal boat down Highway 15. Pamela videos; Tommy drives. He brandishes his penis yet again. Finally, unable to resist, Pamela performs oral sex on Tommy. He operates the camera with his left hand and drives with his right. But Pamela's work is interrupted when Tommy exclaims, "I'm fucking just totally not driving at all! Fuck! Damn, baby."

At length, they pull over onto the shoulder to finish. Sadly, the camera does not join them. Pamela throws a soiled tissue out the window before they hit the road again, showing flagrant disregard for the law.

When the Lees reach their destination, more reckless, naked boating ensues. Pamela says, "You're the best fucking husband on the planet."

Tommy honks the boat horn with his penis. Then he honks Pamela with it, on deck. All we see, for the most part, is out-of-focus genitalia shot in extreme closeup by the shaky cam.

The money shot, as it were, occurs below deck. It's not clear who's operating the camera, but as Tommy finishes his onanistic act, he poignantly says, "Fuck, baby!" "I love you," Pamela says.

Then we cut to footage of the Lees surfing the Web on a Powerbook. Then Tommy scans the cove where they've anchored, declaring the scenery "insane." Then he videos Pamela and, expanding his directorial repertoire, tilts the camera upside down. He says, "Baby, you're upside down." The video ends shortly thereafter.

As a measure of how thoroughly unengaging this presentation is, my wife was out of town for the three days that I had the tape in my possession. And I still screened it only once.

I'm Agile, and I Wear Loose Jeans

"**W**ho's this?"

"My name's Tim. What's your name?"

"Ashleigh." [I'm guessing, obviously, on the spelling.]

"Is that your real name, Ashleigh?"

"[laughing] Why do you say that, Tim?"

"Oh, I don't know. I guess I'm a skeptic."

"You're a skeptic?"

"Uh-huh [wondering how much the effort to establish her real name has already cost me]."

"Well, yes, my name is Ashleigh, and I'm in California."

"Interesting. I'm in Dallas."

"Work out there?"

"Well, I try to work, yes. And this is my first phone sex call."

"This is, like, my third."

"[laughing like I've heard that one before, even though I haven't] It's your third? Really. So, uh, so how do we begin?"

"Well, I had a good time on the phone last time."

"Did ya?"

"Yeah, I got to know this particular person, and he told me a little about himself and what he did and where he was from. And, I don't know, one thing led to another. He sounded gorgeous. So maybe you could tell me what you look like and what you like to do for fun."

"All that sounds like it would get very expensive if I started describing myself in detail."

"Well, you can tell me your height and weight and what size cock you have."

"I'm 6 feet tall, and I weigh 170 pounds. And, uh, I don't know. I guess my, my cock is probably average size [laughing because, strangely enough, telling a woman whose real name I'm fairly sure I don't know that I have an average-size cock, over the phone, is embarrassing]."

"[laughing] What's average? I don't have a cock chart."

"You've read the Kinsey report, right? Whatever average is."

"[really having a hearty chuckle] You are so funny, Tim!"

"Uh-huh. So how big are your genitalia?"

"[chuckling] Well, I have 36B breasts, and my butt is a 32."

"Is it? And do you have big feet?"

"No. What's big? I wear a 6 1/2."

"Gotcha. [pause] So this is probably like a cliché-type question, but what are you wearing?"

"Well, I have on a tank top. And thong underwear."

"And those would be, like, smalls?"

"No. Mine are medium."

"Do they let you try those on before you buy them, or is that the sort of thing where you just need to know your size when you buy it?"

"They don't let you try on panties in the store."

"Do they let you try on bras? I haven't bought too many bras, myself, is why I ask."

"Do you have a girlfriend?"

"Uh, actually I have a wife, yeah."

"[pause] Does she take you shopping?"

"Sure, but usually I wait outside so that it makes her feel guilty and makes her shop more quickly. It's gets her in and out. A little double entendre there for you."

"[pause that I estimate cost me 34 cents] Oh. [15-cent pause] So, okay, tell me, what do you have on?"

"I'm not wearing any shoes, actually. I wear a size 10, in case you're curious. And I got a pair of bluejeans on and a pullover shirt. And, uh, a pair of boxers. All-cotton. Size large. Oh, and I have a watch on, too."

"[laughing nervously] What's the watch for?"

"You got to keep track of time. Know what I'm saying? A little fiscal responsibility."

"[laughing, which is beginning to wear thin] Okay, well, tell me this. Can I at least get you to take off the jeans?"

"[guessing how long it takes to shed bluejeans, but not wanting to overestimate because let's remember the clock is running] Alright, I got my jeans off."

"That fast?"

"I'm agile, and I wear loose jeans."

"Did you take your shoes off?"

"I wasn't wearing any shoes. See? You're not listening very closely."

"[laughing nervously] Okay, I'm sorry, I'm sorry."

"You know, I'll tell you what. My wife is about to get out of the bath, so I'm going to head off."

"Why you got to go?"

"She's going to get out of the bath here, and it's getting late."

"Well, okay. It was nice speaking with you."

"Okay."

"Bye."

Don't Say Anything During Sex Unless You Want Your Man to Repeat It

TODAY, I ADDRESS THE WOMENFOLK IN THE HOUSE. NORMALLY I tailor my messages for the men, because I am a man, and we men generally see eye to eye on certain issues, such as Mark McGwire (bad-ass) and urethroscopy (totally not bad-ass). So I can say something like, "Roger Maris played fewer games, but I would not enjoy a urethroscopy, even if Mark McGwire performed the procedure," and guys will all pretty much agree with me. Preaching to the choir, they call it.

But today, like I said, I have something to impart to the distaff members of the congregation. Something you ladies should know. A piece of advice you would be well-served follow. That advice is this: Do not talk dirty during sex — at least not during sex with men. Maybe lesbians are different. I don't know. I haven't had much experience with postcoital lesbians, so I can't say. But I do know about postcoital men, and believe me: They share.

Like the other day, for example. My friend was relating to several assembled chums, unsolicited, the details of an evening he'd shared with a special lady friend of his. To protect his identity, I'll call my friend Smike.

"You should have heard her," Smike said. And then, because he apparently meant it, that we *should* have heard her, and because he knew, obviously, that we hadn't, he did his best impression, raising his voice an octave: " 'Oh, Smike, give it to me. I want it *soo* bad. I want your hard [vulgar slang for male intromittent organ] in my [pussy]. Oooh, baby, give it to me. Yes. I'm so dirty. Yes, I am. Yes, yes, yesyesyes. And I'm bad. Teach me a lesson, *El Jefe.*' "

Smike is good at doing impressions. I can speak for the group when I say he really put us in the scene.

Now, a few quick words here to the chatty, bilingual woman who is shagging a friend of mine and who thinks she has decoded my nom de plumbery and who is right now picking up the phone to ask her brothers, tearfully, to fit me for a Colombian necktie: Relax, my pretty little nasturtium. Any resemblance of the details contained herein to your sex life is purely coincidental. And, besides, I'm talking about that *other* chatty, bilingual woman who's shagging my *other* friend, whose anonym, Smike, I generated using a highly sophisticated algorithm that you couldn't have possibly decoded.

Anyway, so the point is, guys are not exactly what you'd call sensitive about this stuff. They love to relate tales of their sexual exploits. Telling butt stories, they call it. I guess men do this because — not to put too fine a point on it — telling butt stories is fun. Way more fun than urethroscopies.

Guys also like to bestow nicknames. I am not aware of a single instance in which guys have nicknamed a girl and the nickname was flattering. Smike's girl's actual name was something hard to remember — like, Jill, I think. But by the denouement of Smike's story, as the girl blued the air in earnest with her increasingly specific requests as to where and how Smike should give it to her, one of our group had renamed that poor, unfortunate lass The Jiz Singer (those not familiar with the history of motion pictures will not get this joke and will need to ask a smart person to explain it to them).

Me, I'm not like other guys. My group of friends only lets me hang with them because I know this guy who has a pickup truck that he lets me borrow sometimes to help someone move.

So I asked Smike, "How do you do it? I mean, I know how you *do it*. I've done it plenty of times. But how do you keep a straight ... that is, how do you keep from laughing when The Jiz Singer is carrying on like that?"

"If a girl asked me to put my elbow in her ass and bark like a dachshund while she read aloud the raunchiest parts from *What to Expect When You're Expecting*, I'd be all over it," Smike told me.

"Hitting that coochie, they call it."

"Precisely," Smike said. "It's not till after I'm done that I go, 'Oh, wait a minute. You're gross.' Then I can't wait to tell you guys about it."

So listen to me, ladies, and know that I speak the truth. Movies without dialogue don't do well at the box office. Guys hate artsy-fartsy flicks. If you must, block out the scene before you begin, but don't say anything during sex unless you want your man repeating it. If you can't keep your mouth shut, try lesbianism.

The First One Always Has a Toehold
on the Gray Matter

I WAS MAXING AND RELAXING AT AN AREA "GROG HAUS" THAT SERVES something like 157 beers on tap. I had just ordered a Schadenfreude Extra Special Bitter Clear and was standing at the bar, trying to look as if I weren't trying to look cool and insouciant — but also possibly dangerous — when I heard the voice.

Blonde, port side: "Hi, Tim."

I hate this. People are always saying, "Hi, Tim," when they damn well know I don't know who they are — or, worse yet and more frequently, when I *do* know who they are but can't recall their names. I've tried that vegetamnemonic device wherein you visualize, say, a cucumber protruding from someone's forehead when you meet him, the idea being that you'll associate his name with the cucumber so that when you next meet him, you'll see the imaginary forehead-mounted cucumber and go, "Cucumber ... cucumber ... Ned!"

See but the catch is, first you have to remember the cucumber. You know? Substituting a vegetable for a name is kind of like giving up chiva for GHB. Neither does much for the old long-term potentiation.

So I frequently find myself shaking hands with someone and thinking, "Turnip? Rutabaga? I know this bastard's a crucifer."

Well, I didn't even have a family for this girl's vegetable. I stared hard at her forehead. Concentrated. Got nothing. I am not gifted at faking my way through such encounters and finally said, "Hello, you deranged harpy whom I've never met and with whom I hope to suffer as brief an exchange as possible so that you can return to the lair from whence you came and I can return to my Schadenfreude Extra Special Bitter Clear" — only without that last part about the deranged harpy.

"It's Janet," she said. And that's all it took.

Janet was the girl who broke the stay-fresh seal on my jar of gametes. Served as test pilot on the maiden voyage of my dirigible of diddling. Popped my cherry.

I was 16 and by that time badly burdened by my virginity. The evening of our first meeting, orchestrated by a mutual friend, saw the two of us naked and harboring concupiscent thoughts in a Jacuzzi-brand hot tub maintained by the residents of a gated community to which neither of us belonged (you know how these things happen). But before our efforts could bring about any sort of satisfying resolution, a flashlight-wielding security guard showed up to secure the hot tub, and I wound up standing, dripping wet, Jacuzzi-side, tumescent, trying to mumble my way out of trouble while wearing the first thing I could grab, Janet's size-4 shorts. I am not now, nor was I then, a size 4.

The evening of our second meeting, oddly enough, saw us again in a hot tub, this one owned by her own personal parents and populated, additionally, by two colleagues of mine. We (Janet and I) eventually repaired to an indoor floor, where the deed was done. The next day, I learned that I had had some assistance in priming Janet's pump from one of my chums. He had watched too many episodes of *Man From Atlantis*, but his feet, apparently, weren't webbed, because in the hot tub, underwater, he had surreptitiously worked his big toe, past the knuckle, into Janet.

Like I said, that's all it took. She spoke her name, and it clicked. Janet. Jacuzzi Janet. The first one always has a toehold, as it were, on the gray matter. I remembered it all. Our moment on the floor had taken place more than a dozen years ago. I hadn't seen her since. And Janet no longer looked a size 4 (which, for some perverse reason, I took joy in). But I remembered it all.

"You'll never guess who I've been married to for five years," she said, choosing that, I suppose, over, "Hey, remember that time when we were 16, and I screwed you on my parents' floor?"

I couldn't guess to whom she'd been married for five years. She told me his name. I couldn't recall who he was — no forehead even on which to picture a vegetable. Are you married? she asked. Two years, I said.

And then we reached that moment when things were going to get awkward, and I told Janet, "Well, hey, it's been great seeing you. After your riding my friend's toe in the hot tub and then me on the floor — for which I will forever owe you a debt of gratitude, because if you hadn't taken pity on me, God knows when I would have gotten laid — I never expected to see you again." Only without that last part about the riding.

I took my Schadenfreude to my table and drank to Janet.

Fat People, Minorities, Cripples, and Queers

800 Pounds Is Simply Overdoing It

AT THE RISK OF SOUNDING INSENSITIVE, I HAVE TO ASK: WHAT IS the deal, exactly, with the fat people?

And I don't mean the overweight people. Overweight I can understand. You've got your overweight epicureans who eat veal for breakfast because it's part of their personal philosophy and you've got your overweight African tribesmen who nourish their avoirdupois as a sign of prosperity and you've got your overweight housewives from Duncanville who drive sports utility vehicles as a sign of prosperity and who are a size 20 basically due to laziness. I'm down with those folks.

It's the fat people I don't get. The people who weigh, like, 700 pounds. The people who make it on television. Because I'm watching *Inside Edition* the other day, when Deborah Norville comes on after a commercial break with this real concerned look on her face and introduces a segment about this seriously fat guy up in Pennsylvania who weighs in excess of 800 pounds and who has been unable to leave his house for years.

As an aside, what's up with that perky Deborah Norville? Remember when she landed the anchor spot at *Inside Edition* a couple years back, and everyone was riding her butt 24-7 about selling out? And remember how Deborah kept iterating how she was a "newswoman" and she intended to raise the bar over at *Inside Edition* and do "serious stories"? Well, it occurs to me that the super fat man isn't exactly the war in Bosnia.

But so this guy named Tom in Pennsylvania is the kind of fat that requires emergency rescue personnel to tear down a wall of Tom's house because Tom's level of prosperity has grown to the point where it's only a matter of time before Tom's internal organs are crushed under his own weight. Apparently Tom has been lying in bed for years, which is understandable, because I think if I weighed 800 pounds, I'd hole up in bed, too. Plus, you know, he physically can't move. Also understandable. Tom just lies there, eating and drinking and watching television and trying to breathe. No word on sex, but I'm guessing you can pretty much rule that out.

The *Inside Edition* cameras reveal that Tom favors Wild Turkey, as there are multiple empty bottles within reach. No mention of who's bringing Tom his hooch, since he can't exactly secure his own. He's got a walking cane he uses to push the buttons on his bedside microwave. Nurses have been visiting Tom every so often to attend to his needs, which can't be pleasant, given Tom's logistic problems with elimination and the general horniness that tends to build up when you do nothing but lie around in bed for a few years, drinking Wild Turkey.

In come the emergency rescue personnel to save Tom for the *Inside Edition* cameras. They chain-saw directly through his bedroom wall. About 10 guys load Tom onto a forklift, drive him across his front yard, with stunned neighbors looking on, and onto a flatbed truck. Tom is trucked to the hospital, where, presumably, doctors will reduce his Wild Turkey intake in an effort to save his organs.

And the part I really don't understand is when Deborah Norville comes back on with that same doe-eyed look of total and complete compassion and says, "What an inspirational story. We wish Tom success, and our prayers are with him."

Come on, Tom weighs 800 pounds! He drank himself fat! And that's not easy to do, because dedicated drunks usually lose their appetite and eat about one slice of white bread, total, per day.

Look, I know God loves the super fat people, too, and that many of them wind up in their state of enormity due to psychological illness et cetera. Fine, I'll spot you 400 pounds. Hell, if you're suffering really nasty memories of childhood abuse, go ahead and balloon up to 500 pounds. But 800 pounds is simply overdoing it. You might, as a tax-paying citizen, be entitled to an in-home emergency rescue, but not to sympathy.

It's like the surprisingly large number of people every year who accidentally kill themselves by autoerotic asphyxiation. These people, in my book, get what they deserve. This is natural selection. If you're discovered hanging naked from the rafters, with skin magazines and tubes of petroleum jelly lying at your feet, then you warrant mockery — not prayer.

So to all the fat people out there: Five hundred pounds is my sympathy threshold. Get any fatter, and don't expect me to pray for you. There are people more deserving who are not only starving but doing it at the hands of Sally Struthers.

And to Deborah Norville: Get a job.

It's a Thirsty Nation

I WAS STANDING IN LINE AT 7-ELEVEN RECENTLY, WHEN I SAW SOMETHING that jarred loose a bit of animal-husbandry trivia from one of the back shelves of my brain.

The factoid concerned turkey farming. Modern-day turkey farmers have to inseminate their hens artificially. This is because gobblers have been selectively bred over the years for the size of their breasts, the most commercially desirable body part. Their breasts have now gotten so unnaturally large that the gobblers can't copulate with the hens (or "tread upon" them, as we say in the bird business). In mascot terms, think of it as the Michelin Man trying to have sex with one of the Laker girls.

What I saw in 7-Eleven that made me think of turkeys screwing was a plump woman getting a Double Gulp of Diet Coke. She had to use both hands to carry it to the counter. The Double Gulp is that large. It is 64 ounces of liquid refreshment and weighs upwards of 4 pounds when full.

Never mind what the woman was thinking when she got 64 ounces of *diet* beverage. I mean, it would be my first inclination, if I were looking to loose some pounds, to drink water or possibly even settle for 16 ounces of regular Coke instead of four times that volume of diet. But maybe the woman had a healthy self-image and was unfazed by the barrage of light-beer commercials featuring anorexic bikini-clad women who fill men with unrealistic expectations. (Although, I doubt it.)

No, what struck me about the woman's Double Gulp was its sheer size and that she had to carry it with two hands. The beverage cup, I understood at that moment, has been bred beyond the point of usefulness. The vessel technicians at 7-Eleven have wrought a drink so unnaturally large that it cannot easily be carried. What you've got here, literally, is a convenience store selling inconvenient beverages.

As a concerned citizen and enemy of all things unnatural, I called the folks at Southland Corporation, the parent company of 7-Eleven, to tell them it's not nice to fool with Mother Nature. I got Karen Raskopf, spokeswoman, on the phone.

Karen is a woman who understands the intricacies of beverage container design and isn't afraid to speak her mind. First, she lectured me on the history of 7-Eleven cup evolution.

"When we came out with the 32-ounce Big Gulp in 1980," she said, "people outside of our company and inside our company were saying people would never drink that much liquid. But it sold phenomenally well."

So she claimed that when 7-Eleven came out with the 44-ounce Super Big Gulp five years later, they were just trying to satisfy demand. Yeah, right. Then how do you explain the advent of the Double Gulp in 1988? Surely the Super Big Gulp was enough to do the job.

Apparently not, according to Karen. Even after having to reinvent the cup each time they came out with a new size because larger volumes of liquid required sturdier, longer-lasting cups, the 7-Eleven refreshmentologists have determined that the two largest cup sizes sell the best. Karen said the exact figures were top secret, proprietary information, but she did go on record by saying, "A vast percentage of sales are of the two largest sizes."

Vast percentage, she said.

I did some checking of my own. I asked around the office, and I could find only one co-worker who had ever gotten a Double Gulp. And she only bought it because she was "extremely hung over" and experiencing a bad case of the jicks, which probably prevented her from thinking clearly. Plus, she couldn't finish it.

Karen became very defensive when I told her about my co-worker and suggested the Double Gulp wasn't popular and might even be a clever scheme to fatten us up. .

"Believe it or not," she said, "we get regular calls telling us that if we'd come out with a bigger size, they'd drink it. If we get enough calls on it, I never can tell what those wild and crazy people in merchandising will come up with."

I'll tell you what the wild and crazy people in merchandising will come up with: the 96-ounce Death Gulp! The beverage that will soak us into complacency and make us slow, easy targets.

Karen tried to confuse me with doublespeak and convoluted theories about the trend toward larger cups. She rattled off something about ice-to-soda ratios and self-service beverage bars and said cheerfully, "Especially in the summertime, you're going to see people getting a bigger drink and using more ice.

"People just like to have their liquids," she said, as if it were that simple. "It's a thirsty nation."

Or maybe we're gobblers headed to slaughter, and the farmer's screwing our hens.

As of 1990, There Were 11 Eskimo People Living in Dallas

'VE GOT A PROBLEM. I JUST REALIZED ALL MY FRIENDS ARE AS WHITE AS Liquid Paper. Most folks, if someone calls them a racist, can say, "I'm not a racist. Some of my best friends are black." Point being, if you've got some black friends, then absolutely no way whatsoever at all can you be a racist.

But not me. I don't expect it to happen, but if someone should call me a racist, I can't deny it and offer as proof my black friends, because I don't have any. Not a single one.

I do have one Mexican friend and one Chinese friend, but they're married to each other, and besides, I've never heard anyone say, "I'm not a racist. Some of my best friends are Chinese."

Now I do *know* two black people. If we saw each other in the grocery store, we'd say hi and stop to chat about the weather or whatever. But we're not exactly what I'd call friends. I wouldn't ask either one of the black people I know to help me move or even to come over for a swim in my pool.

Not that I'm trying to suggest black people can't swim or that they don't like the water. I believe black people can swim just as well as white people can play basketball. Black people also make fine hockey players and golfers. It's just that the two black people I know, I don't know well enough to invite over for a swim.

So I started wondering why I don't have any black friends. My first thought was that Dallas simply has a dearth of black people to invite over for a swim. But it turns out that's not true.

According to the 1990 census, in the city of Dallas there are 297,018 black people who could be my friend. Of course, since 1990, some of them have died or moved to another city, but it's safe to say that there are somewhere around 300,000 black people in Dallas who have never been in my pool.

I don't get this. I also learned that, as of 1990, there were 11 Eskimo people living in Dallas. It makes sense that I don't have any Eskimo friends, because with so few around, the chances of even meeting one — not to mention getting one in my pool — are slimmer than Jim. But with so many black people living in Dallas, it would seem difficult not to have a few of them as friends.

Well, I thought, maybe there are so many white people in Dallas that there aren't enough black friends to go around. But I found out that's not true, either. The 1990 census says there are 353,245 white people in Dallas (not including Hispanics, which, for some reason, the census considers white), meaning that there is about .84 of a black for each white person. Assuming that some of the white people in Dallas *are* racists and don't want to have a black friend, and taking into account that I'm a personable fellow, I should have *at least* one black friend and perhaps as many as three or four.

Then I dug a little deeper into the 1990 census, and it all began to make sense. I found that only five percent of the people within my 75206 ZIP Code are black, which works out to only around .11 of a black per white person, which explains a few things.

If you've ever been sitting in a Lower Greenville-area restaurant and gotten the feeling that everybody else looks *exactly* like you, there's a good reason. Namely, everybody else looks exactly like you.

And my neighborhood looks like a Benetton melting pot filled with a racial soup you could eat with a fork compared to some other nearby ZIP Codes. Over in 75205, the Park Cities area, you have to look very hard to find black people, and one suspects the task becomes nearly impossible when daylight fades and lawn care stops.

Basically, painting with broad brush-strokes, there's a line that divides Dallas. Depending on which side of the Trinity River you live, you either swim with black people or white people. And it cannot be overlooked that there are more pools on the northern side.

For someone like me who makes a living spewing viewpoints, this arrangement is less than ideal. Forget that I don't have a trite defense should someone call me a racist; by not not having any black friends, I'm missing out on material. There are viewpoints I'll never hear and a culture I'll never experience.

I can't help but wonder if there's someone living in ZIP Code 75215 or 75217 who feels the same way I do. Maybe a guy in South Dallas or Pleasant Grove wishes he had a white friend. Maybe he suspects he's missing out on something.

But neither of us will probably find out, because I live here and he lives there, and never the twain shall meet.

Bob Dole Doesn't Like It When People Offer Their Right Hands to Shake

I AM A WHITE BOY AND SO I AM NOT SUPPOSED TO THINK THOUGHTS like this, and even if I do think thoughts like this, propriety would require that I keep them to myself. Nevertheless, here is the thought: Bob Dole should get himself a black friend.

Let me explain. The other day, I ran into a black guy I know. I don't know many black people (I hope this doesn't make me a bigot), so the chances of my running into one I recognize are slim indeed. But there he was, walking across a parking lot. I pulled up and rolled down my window.

"Hey, man," I said. (I say, "Hey, man," to white people, too. Please don't think I was trying to sound "street" or "down" or whatever.)

Charles — that was the black guy's name, Charles — he leaned into my car, on the passenger-side door. We chitchatted. I don't remember what about. Sports, the weather, stuff like that. At length, it came time to say goodbye.

That's when Charles offered me his fist. He stuck it out there, fingers clenched, thumb part up, as if he were holding a length of rope. Except there wasn't any rope.

I thought, *What should I do with this fist?* A few awkward fractions of a second passed. I considered shaking his fist, grabbing it like a gear shift and moving it up and down. *Or maybe,* I thought, *I should make a fist, touch the front of my fingers to his, and say, "Wonder twin powers, activate! Form of a snow cone!"*

In the end, I just stuck out my fist, near his, and let Charles lead. He gently hammered the top of my fist like he was trying to fix an electrical appliance that he knew he shouldn't be hammering on. I hammered back with considerably less aplomb.

I'm not sure if it is done intentionally to keep white people a few years behind on handshaking trends, but black people are continually inventing new ways to shake hands. (I don't mean that to sound racist.) Back in the '70s, a black friend of mine showed me how to shake by grasping the fat part of his thumb, like we were about to arm-wrestle. That was state of the art back then.

In the late '80s, another black friend helped me update my method, teaching me how to slide my hand out of a stiff-fingered handshake and make a snapping noise against my palm. I liked that technique. Adding an auditory element to the handshake struck me as genius.

The snap, though, is now out. As Charles demonstrated, the fist hammer is in.

And that is why Bob Dole should get himself a black friend. (Not to suggest that black friends are objects to be acquired.) Dole, as I'm sure you're aware, has a game right arm as a result of having participated in World War II. The game arm makes it hard for him properly shake hands like a white boy.

Now, according to *Emily Post's Etiquette* (Harper Collins, 1992), "When you meet someone whose right arm or hand is missing or is deformed, extend your right hand even though he or she cannot shake hands in the normal way. The handicapped person will appreciate that you have made no unnatural gesture to accommodate his or her disability. He or she will respond by offering his or her left hand, or by saying, 'Please forgive me if I don't shake hands, but I'm very glad to meet you.'"

But Bob Dole must not read Emily Post. He doesn't like it when people offer their right hands to shake. In fact, Dole often carries an ink pen in his right hand to avoid having to shake with the maladroit. Joe Klein wrote in *Newsweek* that, for years, he had proffered Dole his right hand, and, for years, Dole never once said, "Please forgive me if I don't shake hands, but I'm very glad to meet you." Instead, Dole always gave Klein bad interviews. When Klein finally proffered his left hand, Dole immediately warmed to him.

All of which could have been avoided had Dole spent more time with, say, Jesse Jackson or Colin Powell. Both men, I would bet, are practitioners of the fist-hammer handshake, which requires very little manual dexterity. Even with his deformed hand, Dole could hammer with confidence.

Mr. Dole, if you're reading, please hammer, but don't hurt 'em.

Not All Black People Are Smart

TODAY'S LESSON IS AN IMPORTANT ONE, SO LISTEN UP. SOMEWHERE along the line, we as a nation forgot something. I can't pinpoint exactly when our collective memory failed, but it threatens to tear this country apart. What we forgot is this:

Some black people are stupid.

Actually, we seem to have lost track of an entire body of knowledge. We have also forgotten that some Chinese people are stupid, some Mexican people are stupid, and some white people are stupid.

It's important that everyone understands these truisms, and long-forgotten knowledge sometimes sinks in slowly. So let's go over a few of the finer points.

First, let's not quibble over terms. Many modern-day scholars argue that the term "stupid" is a vulgar idiom not to be used in a proper sociological discussion. Such scholars are stupid. Our forefathers used the word "stupid" liberally. And rightfully so. It is a fine, sturdy, old-fashioned word that gets the job done. We need not distinguish between "stupid" and "ignorant." Forget about "disadvantaged" or "differently abled" or any of that other mince-minded codswallop.

It is best to keep matters simple and straightforward, and so we will say that some black people — and Chinese and Mexican and white people — are stupid.

Next, let's address the designation "some." A colleague of mine is of the opinion that *most* black people are stupid. Indeed, he believes that most people, as a whole, are stupid. This would include Mexican and Chinese and white people, among others.

I disagree. I have more faith in humanity than does my colleague. We have landed a man on the moon and are on the verge of giving federal approval to the first genuinely delicious calorie-free fat substitute. With progress like that, I refuse to believe that most black people are stupid or even that *many* black people are stupid. If we are to err, let us do it on the conservative side of the estimate and say that some black people — and Chinese and Mexican and white people — are stupid.

For those students in the class who still refuse to accept that some black people are stupid and for those who are having a difficult time grasping the concept (the stupid students), I offer as final proof that some black are stupid this syllogism: Not all people are smart; black people are people; therefore not all black people are smart, which means some are stupid.

I am writing this on the blackboard. Put it in your notes. It will be on the test.

At this juncture, many of you are probably thinking, *Your theory is all well and fine, professor, but how does it work outside of the classroom? How can I take what I've learned and apply it to real-life situations?* Excellent question.

Let us suppose a stupid black person — or Chinese or Mexican or white person — is a teller at a bank, and she cannot count. She gets as high as 14, but then forgets what comes next and has to start over again. Also, she can't add or subtract.

This causes problems at the bank. Customers complain about receiving incorrect change and having to remind the stupid black person that after 14 comes 15. So the teller's boss, who is Chinese, fires the wrong-change-making, no-arithmetic-doing, stupid black person.

Let us further suppose that the next day, the "African-American community" pickets the bank for being a racist institution. One of the more vocal protesters calls the Chinese boss a racist and a banana, meaning she's yellow on the outside but white on the inside.

Here, attentive pupils, is how you can apply what you have learned in class today: Unlike the vocal protester, you will understand that some black people are stupid. You will realize that sometimes stupid black people — and Chinese and Mexican and white people — get fired and that when they get fired, it is because of their stupidity, not because they are black.

Furthermore, you will know that if the vocal protester loses favor with the "Chinese community" or anyone else, it is because he called a Chinese person a banana, not because he is black. And it will most certainly be nothing like apartheid.

Alright. Class dismissed. Your assignment for next week's class is to read *The Content of Our Character*, by Shelby Steele, who is, by the way, a very smart black person.

Monica Seles?
Lesbian.

LAST WEEK AT WORK, WHEN MY *TIME* MAGAZINE ARRIVED, THE ONE with Ellen DeGeneres crouching on the cover, saying, "Yep, I'm gay," I had to beat the lesbians off with a stick. Not literally. I didn't actually hit the lesbians in my office with a stick, because hitting lesbians — or normal women, for that matter — is unacceptable (nowadays). Which is not to suggest that lesbians aren't normal. Because lesbians are normal. That's not what I'm saying at all.

Anyway, I work with a handful lesbians, all of whom are perfectly normal people. Well, one of them is sort of weird, but her weirdness is completely unrelated to her lesbianism. But when those lesbians saw that *Time* in my mailbox with Ellen DeGeneres crouching on the cover, they snatched that sucker up like it was the last cucumber at the salad buffet. And I don't mean that as a double entendre. That would be wrong.

I found the lesbians all standing around together, reading my *Time*. I said, "Hey, is that my *Time*? Did you snatch that out of my box?"

One of the lesbians said, "I stole it, but I just wanted to read this article about Ellen DeGeneres. She is coming out, you know. It says so right here on the cover. 'Yep, I'm gay.' "

And then one of the other lesbians said, "As if that's not obvious from the way she's crouching. Like she's a catcher or something, squatting down behind the plate, giving the signal for a split-fingered, off-speed pitch. 'Hey, batter, batter! Swing batter!' "

Another lesbian said, "Plus, look at those white shoes she's wearing. Those are lesbian loafers if I ever saw them. I bet she borrowed those loafers from her father. 'Is the photo shoot over? Because my dad said to have his loafers back before 10.' "

Lesbians are pretty funny. At least the lesbians I know are pretty funny. I wouldn't want to make a blanket statement like "all lesbians are funny." Because that's not true. I'm sure there are plenty of dull lesbians out there. But the lesbians at my work are funny gals. And I know the word "gal" is supposed to be demeaning to women, but I'm pretty sure the lesbians in my office wouldn't mind being called "gals." They are a rough-and-ready bunch, those lesbians. And I mean that as a compliment.

Well, by this time, a whole group of people had gathered around the lesbians who were reading my *Time* magazine with Ellen DeGeneres crouching on the cover in her clunky loafers, saying, "Yep, I'm gay." There were some straight women and straight guys. No gay guys, though. I'm not sure, but I don't think any homosexual men work in my office. Although I guess it's possible and I just don't know it. We don't discriminate against homosexuals where I work. I mean, we've got lesbians, right?

So one of the straight guys said, "Is Ellen, the actress, gay? Or is Ellen, the character on the show *Ellen*, gay?"

"Both," the lesbians answered in unison.

"And look," a lesbian said. "Laura Dern is going to play Ellen's love interest. Mmm, Laura Dern could come out to me anytime. She is so fine."

That lesbian looked at the picture of Laura Dern in *Time* magazine with a powerful lust in her eyes. I have to admit, as a straight man, the thought of Laura Dern engaging in a little lesbian rock-and-roll hoochie-coochie kind of puts a point on my compass. I mean, I saw *Wild at Heart*, and until she got pregnant and started puking on the floor, Laura Dern was definitely hot. I don't think I'd pick Ellen DeGeneres as her teammate, though. Maybe Jodie Foster.

"Laura Dern is gay?" I said.

"She's at least part gay," one of the lesbians said. "That's the word on the street."

I'd like to believe her, but I think she was making that up about Laura Dern. The lesbians I work with are always assuring me that so-and-so is gay. "That's the word on the street," they'll say. Like there's some underground gay communiqué they all get. "Monica Seles? Lesbian. Read it last week in the newsletter."

The thing is, sometimes they do have inside information. Lily Tomlin, for instance. I had no idea.

Look, the bottom line is this: Lesbians should have to wear a uniform. Gay guys, too. I want to know, at a glance, who's on which team. You know? You've got your Astros and your Rockies. You don't confuse them. Or maybe a tattoo. Just the word "GAY," in capital letters. On their foreheads. I don't do well with ambiguity. That's all I'm saying.

You Are Not Supposed to Use the Word "Gimp"

THE OTHER DAY I HAD AN APPOINTMENT WITH A BUSINESS ASSOCI-ate. I'll call him Henry Kissinger. Henry Kissinger and I had had several cordial, though businesslike, telephone conversations, but we had yet to meet. Never actually pressed the flesh, Henry Kissinger and I.

He sounded to me like a big man. Well over 6 feet. One of those barrel-chested guys with thick wrists. Probably in his early 50s. I envisioned — again, solely from having spoken with him over the telephone — Henry Kissinger wearing dungarees and carrying a well-used machete. He definitely had a mustache.

Imagine my surprise, then, when I arrived on the day of our appointment at Henry Kissinger's office and, after waiting a few minutes in the lobby, discovered that not only did he lack a mus-tache, but Henry Kissinger was a gimp. And a petite one at that.

Oh, right, except I understand that you're not supposed to use the word "gimp." Ditto with the words "cripple" and "mutant" and espe-cially the phrase "circus freak." Just like people don't have leprosy any-more; they have Hansen's disease. I would opt for the medical term for what Henry Kissinger had, but he exhibited such a multitude of teratological discombobulations that I wouldn't know where to begin.

He was swaybacked and wry-necked, clubfooted and knock-kneed. I think he had a wandering eye, but I couldn't bring myself to look him in the face long enough to be certain.

As mentioned, though, he possessed a commanding baritonal voice of the sort you hear in trailers for Merchant Ivory films. So it wouldn't be inaccurate to call Henry Kissinger "differently abled."

Now, I have two problems with people who are profoundly "dif-ferently abled." The first is, I'm curious.

Henry Kissinger slogged up to me there in the lobby — obviously not carrying a machete, because no way could this guy safely walk with even a metal spoon in his claw — and introduced himself. "Hi, Tim, I'm Henry," Henry Kissinger said.

"Pleasure to make your acquaintance," I said, shaking Henry Kissinger's claw. "What's the story with all the deformities?"

At least that's what I wanted to ask. How could you *not* want to know? Like, if you were to meet Siamese twins, could you pretend nothing was out of the ordinary? Of course not. You'd want to ask, right away: "What's up with the two heads?" Put an unsupervised child anywhere in the vicinity of Siamese twins, or just a guy missing a finger, and the child will get to the bottom of the condition. Children aren't afraid to ask. They're curious. It's natural.

Sometimes children also bite other people and drink cleaning agents from under the kitchen sink, but you get my point.

So there's the curiosity, with me, about the specific nature of the birth defect or what have you. That's difficult enough to suppress. Henry Kissinger and I were talking business in the lobby. He was hunched over, listing to starboard, looking like he might tumble into a nearby ficus, and all I could think was, *Don't ask, don't ask.*

But then Henry Kissinger said, "Follow me. I'll introduce you to the rest of the people in the office." And then my second problem with horrifically "differently abled" people came into play.

He made an awkward turn, as if someone standing behind him were holding a rope tied to Henry Kissinger's belt buckle and that someone had yanked on the rope, hard, causing Henry Kissinger's arms to pinwheel. He went limp-lumbering down a hall at several knots slower than my cruising speed, so that, in trying not to stare at him — in other words, looking over his head, down the hall, or to the left and right — I twice almost ran into Henry Kissinger. I couldn't walk alongside him, due to his erratic, side-to-side gait. So to avoid rear-ending Henry Kissinger and to maintain proper separation, I had to downshift and watch him closely.

My second problem is this: If a "differently abled" person manifests his non-ability in even a mildly humorous way, I have a compulsion to imitate it. Especially when it comes to silly walks. You know Monty Python's Ministry of Silly Walks? When I was younger, I spent hours mastering them all and trying to invent my own.

With a little effort, I can keep my curiosity at bay. My compulsion to imitate is far stronger. I realize this hardly passes for a defense of my actions, nonetheless …

Henry Kissinger was in the lead, all over the road. Oncoming traffic had to stand aside and let us pass. He was swinging his arms dangerously and dragging his right foot like he'd stepped in chewing gum and was trying to scrape it off. His left foot's action was even worse. He was hell on his shoes.

And I followed. Closely, slowly. Watching him walk. Almost in tears. Let's just say that, while I doubt Henry Kissinger and I will enjoy a long and mutually beneficial business relationship, I've nearly nailed his walk.

Tony Robbins Hates Excellence

NORMALLY I'M NOT THE KIND OF GUY WHO ATTENDS A TONY Robbins Competitive Edge seminar, which, if you're not familiar with the concept, is a 12-hour painfully high energy pep talk to help you increase your Power of Personal and Professional Influence. Normally I'm the kind of guy who's more concerned with getting Personally and Powerfully Under the Influence. But my boss had an extra $300 ticket, and he said I could take Thursday off to attend.

So here I am at the Dallas Market Hall, sitting in what looks like a blue-draped airplane hangar with 3,000 seriously Type A professionals, waiting for Tony to take the stage, and listening to Marky Mark at bowel-disturbing volume. Business-attired, synchronized dancers warm up the audience, exhorting us to stand and clap. I stand but decline to clap, because let's just say I'm not a huge fan of Marky Mark.

And then Tony jogs out. He is wearing a microphone attached to his head by a means I cannot discern. Tony has a disease called gigantism. He's 6-foot-7 and growing, and even from where I'm sitting, I can tell his hands are absolutely enormous. He claps kind of like a retard.

And so Tony launches into the Competitive Edge seminar, and I'm immediately impressed with how he uses the phrase "and shit" with total aplomb, as in, when he mocks the business-attired warmup dancers, he says, "So what's up with all this dancing and shit?"

Tony tells us that he hates excellence. He loathes it, in fact. Tony's all about the level above "excellent," which is "outstanding."

He sheds his suit coat. He has already sweat clear through his white, French-cuffed shirt. When he slaps his chest, which is Tony's Power Move and something he does a lot, like when he says, "You have to find a way to put yourself" — *slap* — "immediately in a Peak State," you can tell he works out at least once a day and could, without question, kick your ass, retarded clapping style notwithstanding.

No fewer than eight electric fans, some in oscillation mode, blow at Tony from various locations along the periphery of the stage, but the fans do not appear to mitigate Tony's perspiration. When he notices the energy in the room waning, at which he's very accomplished, this energy monitoring, the disturbingly loud music kicks back on, and Tony has us all stand up and scream and execute our own personal Power Moves repeatedly, at Level 30, to put ourselves in a Peak State, and he also has us massage the people seated to our left and right.

Did I mention the workbooks? We each have our own *Competitive Edge* workbooks that function basically like Mad-Libs. There are sentences with blanks in them, which blanks Tony has us fill in with words he gives us, like this: "_Influence_ is the process of getting your client to clearly associate their [sic] most desired feelings, states, or sensations to your product, service, or idea." But I'm outstanding, right? So I work ahead, filling in the blanks before Tony gives us the answers. I fill in "Nothing sells like _____ " with "_hot pie_." This turns out to be incorrect.

During a Peak State induction session, Tony throws T-shirts into the audience. The shirts are rolled up, and Tony has impressive range. The prospect of catching a free shirt, thrown personally by Tony, drives the audience way beyond Level 30, state-wise. Ditto with the Sun Maid raisins in trial-size boxes. I later see a woman holding a bag of ice on a badly swollen black eye. I ask what happened, and she says: "Raisins."

But the most unsettling occurrence of the day — and I didn't realize this until much later — is that Tony gets to me. He gets inside my head. At some point, I'm not sure when, I go from playing along ironically, cheering with mock enthusiasm as we turn each page of the Mad-Libs workbook, to participating in earnest, not wanting to betray Tony's trust in me as a partner in the quest for the Competitive Edge. I genuinely try to give Tony 110 percent, even though I know it's impossible, a priori, to give more than the full 100 percent. I am yelling, "Wooo! Page 17 rules! A state of passion creates" — *slap* — "peak performance!" I am standing on my chair, clambering over other seminar-goers for T-shirts, T-shirts thrown personally by Tony!

Toward the end of the day, I am picked by a Tony Robbins minion to join a dozen other audience members onstage for a demonstration in the course of which I wind up dancing in front of 3,000 people, unbuttoning my shirt like a stripper, and thrusting my pelvis around with such unbridled enthusiasm that I nearly harm myself. I am not proud of this.

At the office the next day, my boss asks how I liked the seminar. I slap my chest and tell him I'm in a Peak State, not sure at all that I'm kidding.

Adventure

Suddenly I Was Yanking on a Metal Bar
Like I Had Scorpions in My Pants

W E CAN ALL AGREE THAT THE SPACE ALIENS HAVE BEEN MONITORING our television broadcasts for years. The question that still remains — what the government has spent millions of dollars trying to figure out — is which show is the aliens' favorite.

Many scientists have suggested that the space aliens favor *Barney and Friends*, saying that Barney himself may actually be an alien who observes earthlings while disguised as a friendly purple foam dinosaur. This theory fails to account for Barney's having been repeatedly tackled by pranksters during recent public appearances. Surely the space aliens, if they had an agent in the Barney suit, would possess the technology to put a stop to the tacklings.

That's why I don't think the aliens prefer *Barney and Friends*. They've got better taste than that. They demand quality entertainment. Their favorite show, then, must be *American Gladiators*.

This program is 60 action-packed minutes of Lycra and sweat. It defines the genre known as "must-see TV." And as far as a social barometer goes, we couldn't invent a better program to showcase the values we Americans hold most dearly: strength, courage, the ability to dodge tennis balls shot from a pneumatic cannon. Lucky for us the aliens can pick up *American Gladiators*. If they only received Bill Moyers' PBS specials, they would have deemed us worthless wimps and invaded long ago.

I can't tell you how many times I've canceled plans on a Saturday night so I could stay home and watch my favorite gladiator, Jazz, in her sassy little outfit, tear up some chick in the "Whiplash" event. The way Jazz goes after that Dog Bone device makes me want to bark like an angry dog. (The bourbon can do that, too.)

So when I heard that the "smash-hit series *American Gladiators*" was holding open tryouts in Dallas for gladiator contestants and that Jazz herself would be in attendance, I began preparations. Immediately, I placed myself on a strict regimen that included doing 1,000 push-ups a day, eating only foods high in carbohydrates, and abstaining from sex.

Roommate Joe shared my enthusiasm. For his part, he rolled out of bed on the morning of the tryouts and smoked a Marlboro. Roommate Joe's preparations completed, we busted cheeks to the downtown YMCA, ready to do battle for Jazz's love.

By the time we got there, a queue had already formed, winding its way around the block. I suspicioned that we might encounter guys who constantly gulp those high-protein, bulk-building shakes that drowned Joe Piscopo's career. Sure enough, the line of hopeful contestants was an ugly, muscle-bound Spandex snake, and it sounded mad.

The guys in the tail of the line had already been through the try-outs once. The first test of strength, they said, was chin-ups — 22 of them in 30 seconds. As far as Roommate Joe and I could gather, everyone in line was upset with the chin-up judges, who reportedly couldn't count past 19.

For an hour, Roommate Joe and I listened to thoughtful advice on the various tests of speed and strength that one needed to pass in order to become a gladiator. On the 40-yard dash: "Even if your legs are slow, you gotta swing your arms fast. That way, your legs will have to keep up."

Roommate Joe worked the Sunday crossword as we wound our way into the YMCA. He would periodically interrupt with questions like, "Is 'chirlup' a word?"

Then it was time. After filling out some paperwork, 10 of us were led to a gym that was filled with sweaty guys and a few girls, all earnestly grunting with one test or another, in an effort to get on television and entertain the space aliens.

We got a quick rundown on the chin-up rules. Someone said, "Ready, set, go," and suddenly I was yanking on a metal bar like I had scorpions in my pants. Then a whistle blew, and through the dizziness, I could hear someone telling me, "Thanks for trying." I was shown the way out. My tryout lasted 30 seconds.

Outside, Roommate Joe and I compared notes. We took solace in the knowledge that if we combined our chin-ups, we had done the required 22, with even a few to spare. Together, we knew we could be a gladiator. We found strength in each other, and that made the trip downtown worth the effort.

That, and before we left the YMCA, I got to meet Jazz. I shook her hand and asked her what her favorite event was. She said, "Whiplash," and I knew we were meant for each other. Swimming in her dark brown eyes, like they were pools of coffee — except not hot coffee, because that would really hurt — I knew what the space aliens, being more advanced than us, must think when they watch Jazz: "Nice butt ... Uh, huh-huh, huh-huh."

I Found a Perch Where I Could Get a Look Around

THE OTHER DAY IT HIT ME: I COULDN'T REMEMBER THE LAST TIME I'd climbed a tree.

When I was a kid, I would climb just about anything, but especially trees. I remember the sapote tree that grew in our backyard in California. It had a metal squirrel guard around its trunk that sliced through the four fingers on my left hand the first time I tried to climb it. My father had told me only moments earlier that it was sharp and dangerous. It was.

Then we moved to Texas when I was 6, and I learned to climb acorn trees, oaks, and magnolias. My cousins had a pecan tree in their front yard that I one day found myself afraid to come down from because I'd climbed too high. My mom had to come out of the house and talk me down, assuring me the whole way that I could reach the next branch with my foot. I swore when I stood on safe ground that I'd never climb another tree as long as I lived. But I did.

I spent more time in trees than in front of the television, which leads me to suspect that's what's wrong with our kids today: too much staring, not enough climbing.

But, like I said, it hit me the other day that I couldn't remember the last tree I'd climbed. I saw this as a bad sign. Unless you're confined to a wheelchair, any reason you can give for not having recently climbed a tree is a lame one. "It hadn't occurred to me" is the lamest.

The tree in town I remember best is the sprawling mulberry that grew in the backyard of my family's first house in Dallas. I didn't have many friends at first, so I spent entire summer afternoons in that mulberry tree. I'd climb to the top and rock back and forth in its thin branches like a giant metronome. Or I'd sit in the thick limbs that hung over the sidewalk and drop ripe, red mulberries on unsuspecting people as they passed below.

So last week when I decided it was time to go climb a tree, I went back to my old house and rang the doorbell. A woman answered, saying hello from behind the screen door, which she left shut.

"Hi," I said, quickly adding, "I'm not selling anything. I have a weird but very sincere request. I used to live here when I was a little kid and that mulberry tree in your backyard was my favorite climbing tree and I was wondering if you might let me climb it."

There was an awkward pause, during which the woman seemed to struggle with the situation. She asked me to wait and shut the door. Moments later, a small boy opened the door, and his father appeared behind him. Hank was the one who had bought the house from my mother after she and my father divorced and the place got too big for the two of us. Luckily, Hank remembered me.

"You've grown up," he said.

"Well, I've gotten taller. There's no debating that."

"Sure," he said. "You can climb the tree."

Hank showed me through my old house and out to the backyard, which, of course, seemed smaller. And there stood the old mulberry tree. This being October, with winter nearly upon us, there weren't any berries. Hank and his son, Jules, were in the process of remodeling a treehouse, which they had torn down because it had started to warp. But besides that, it was the same mulberry tree I remembered.

Jules scrambled up the tree ahead of me, to show me the way, in case I'd forgotten, which I hadn't. Then I went up, taking it slowly to avoid having to explain to co-workers how I'd broken my arm by falling out of a tree.

"Be careful," Jules told me as I headed for higher territory.

I wanted to say, "*You* be careful, pal. I was playing Tarzan in this tree before you were even a horny thought running through your dad's head." But I was a guest on those limbs, so I held my tongue.

"When there are berries in the tree," I asked Jules, "do you drop them on people?"

"No," he said. "I drop rocks."

Times change.

I continued on and found a perch where I could get a look around. There, next to the tree, at eye level, was the gray slate roof. I remembered crawling into the attic and listening to the mulberry branches scrape the slate when the wind blew.

Down the street, on the corner, I could see the Stop'N Go where I used to hang out with my friend Rodney. We'd steal change from our mothers' purses to buy Super Bubble and play Space Invaders, then Galaga when they got it.

And below me, directly across from my old house, I could see the corner where I stood one day, waiting to cross the street with a bike that had a flat tire. An older boy with a lead pipe came up and, after asking me a few questions I didn't answer, told me to give him the bike. Which I did.

Then I climbed down and, feeling a little silly, thanked Hank for the use of his tree. He said I was welcome and seemed to understand.

We Had Hats.
And We Had a Plan.

A WHILE BACK, ROOMMATE EMERITUS JOE AND I WENT TO THE West End to catch a flick. An au courant fellow, Roommate Joe was wearing his ball cap backward.

Before we got to the box office to buy our tickets, a security guard stopped us and asked Roommate Joe to turn his hat around so the bill faced forward. This sounded like an odd request coming from a security guard, because, to the untrained eye, the orientation of Roommate Joe's hat made the West End Marketplace neither more nor less secure. If Roommate Joe had been wearing an extremely *tall* hat, one that threatened to tip over and possibly injure a shopper, or if he'd been wearing a magic hat that allowed him to shoplift without getting caught, then I could see why a security guard would worry about it. A regular ball cap, though, seemed harmless.

If we hadn't been running late for the movie, we might have demanded the guy's badge number and asked to speak to his superior. Instead, we kept our mouths shut, and Roommate Joe turned his hat around. But we swore to return to the West End when we had more time to find out what the Sam Hill was going on with the Hat Nazis.

Last Thursday, Roommate Joe and I had the time. We had hats. And we had a plan. Here's how it shook out:

3:30 — We enter the marketplace conspicuously wearing our ball caps backward.

3:31 — As we attempt to mount the escalator, a red-shirted security guard says, "Ya'll gonna have to turn your hats around in here." Roommate Joe and I feign bewilderment but turn our hats around.

3:33-3:40 — Given that it is impossible to wear a hat with the bill forward and *exactly* centered and therefore assuming the guards will accept a certain amount of hat rotation as user error, Roommate Joe and I ride the escalators with our hats progressively more askew, attempting to determine at what point a merely crooked hat becomes dangerous.

3:41 — With our hats riding approximately 45 degrees from due forward, another red-shirted security guard, who apparently has been in radio contact with the first guard, approaches us and says, "Now ya'll been told once already about wearing your hats to the front. If you don't turn 'em around, you're gonna have to leave." We straighten our hats and prepare for the second stage of our operation.

3:42-3:50 — Roommate Joe and I have a beer up at the food court.

3:51-4:20 — We play Shaq Attaq pinball in the arcade.

4:21 — Roommate Joe puts on a hat that looks exactly like an adjustable ball cap, except that it has no bill. I put on a purple, red, and blue puffy hat that stands 2 feet tall and has two drooping spires, much like a jester's hat.

4:22-4:29 — As Roommate Joe and I ride the escalators, shoppers are visibly disturbed by my hat, perhaps fearing it will tip over on them. Red-shirted marketplace security guards appear frazzled. A guard tails us at a safe distance while holding a walkie-talkie conference with the rest of the Hat Squad.

4:30 — As Roommate Joe and I dismount the escalator on the second floor, a security guard stops us. He asks me to remove my hat and tells Roommate Joe to turn his around. When Roommate Joe complies, the security guard sees he's been duped and chuckles. When I point out that my hat also doesn't have a bill and ask why I have to remove it, the guard explains, "That hat just ain't normal."

That did it. I asked the guard to see his superiors and the guidelines for what is and is not "normal." He sent me over to the West End Headquarters, where I met Karen Conway-Gelfand, director of marketing and PR, and Paul A. Klooster, director of operations.

Karen and Paul invited me back into a conference room and suffered my silly hat questions like the consummate professionals they are. The reason for the hat policy, they explained, is because the gangs found a way around the bandanna policy.

The Bloods and Crips, who identify themselves with red and blue bandannas respectively, had been causing trouble at the West End — as they had at malls across America — so bandannas were outlawed. Even the conventioneers who came through town a few years back, all of them wearing red bandannas, had to take off their "colors" while in the marketplace.

Instead of bandannas, then, the irrepressible and creative gang members resorted to wearing their hats askew. And that's why, about nine months ago, the West End passed the hat-forward rule.

Which may seem like treating the symptom instead of the cause, but that's what happens when shopping malls are forced to play parents. Stupid gangs.

He Got Me With Some Sort of
Sneaky Kung-Fu Move

I'M A LOVER, NOT A FIGHTER. SO WHEN A BRONCO BOWL OFFICIAL called me at the office and asked if I wanted to fight Guy Mezger, I said, "Who the hell is Guy Mezger, and why would I want to kick his sorry ass?"

It turns out that, besides having a porn star's name, Guy Mezger happens to be Guy "The Sandman" Mezger, a third-degree black belt in chung do kwan, whatever that is. And he won that Ultimate Fighting thing where they don't have any rules and you're allowed to punch the other guy in the testicles. And he's the world heavyweight kick-boxing champion, which I guess might impress some people.

Well, the deal was, Guy also does this stuff called pancration, or "free fighting," which is really popular in Japan, where Guy has his own comic book. The Bronco Bowl will play host to the U.S. debut of free fighting, and the official thought I might want to fight Guy — or just spar around with him or whatever — and then write about it, tell all the kids to go check out "The Battle at the Bowl."

I said fine then. Bring on Guy. I'll bust out the jams on this comic-book kick-boxer punk.

I rounded up two of my hos, Rhonda and Sally Jo, and ricky-ticked it over to the Fitness Factory, where they have a boxing ring and where Guy and I agreed to meet. When we arrived, Guy had some of his own crew in attendance and was regaling them with a story about how he'd only recently mixed it up with some dudes down on Greenville and put them to sleep with his signature Sandman move.

I was like, "Quit trying to impress me, man. I'm on a tight schedule. Let's get to business."

We took off our shirts, and I noticed that Guy had a tan that made him look a lot bigger than he actually was — and ripped. He had what I'd call illusory, tan-induced muscles bulging all over the place, so I wasn't worried much about that. I laughed at the liability waiver and signed it.

Guy laced me up with boxing gloves so that, as he put it, "You won't be afraid to hit me." I was thinking, "Right, comic-book boy. Ooh, please don't shoot me with your sleepy-time energy beam." That was the only safety equipment we used — no headgear or mouthpieces or codpieces or anything. Guy didn't wear gloves because he said he wasn't going to hit me.

But he didn't say he wasn't going to kick me in the face, which he did. And pretty hard, too. In the first of three scheduled two-minute rounds, he got me with some sort of sneaky kung-fu move. I think it was his left foot. My eyes got all teary, and the air in the Fitness Factory must have been dry because my nose started bleeding like a madman.

When I realized what had happened, I said, "He kicked me in the nose! The Sandman kicked me in the nose!"

Sally Jo got a paper towel to sop the blood off my face.

The second round featured Sally Jo and Rhonda yelling, "Hit him! Hit him! Hit him!" I'm pretty sure they were yelling for *me* to hit Guy and not the other way around. But Guy had all these shifty wang-chung moves, and every time I closed in for a punch, he'd go into "free-fight mode" and throw me to the mat and put me in a ninja death hold where I couldn't hit him. One time after he had taken me down, Guy proceeded to give me a world-champion charley horse on my calf, which I was pretty sure was illegal, even in Japan.

I did get in one kick. It was a savage, possibly career-ending shot to Guy's right shin. Only his tan saved him.

In the third round, Guy put his hands down and told me just to go ahead and unload on him, give him all I had. I thought that was pretty weak, considering by the third round I was so winded from breathing through all the blood that I was dizzy and couldn't even gather enough spit to put out a match. When I bum-rushed him with my knockout punch, the right cross of righteous fury, he juked left, and I almost went over the top rope on my follow-through. Then, to end the thing, he put me in another flying feng-shui hold until I manfully said, "Aww! Eee-ouch! Uncle, uncle! I give!"

So, really, it was a close fight. If Guy hadn't used all that Bruce Lee ginsu junk on me, I would have messed him up good, and they'd have to rewrite comic-book history over in Japan. As it was, though, Guy managed to escape with his butt still intact. Unless my posse and I catch him down in the 'hood, on Greenville, he'll be healthy enough to participate in the World Free-Fight Championships at the Bronco Bowl. If you're into that sort of thing, I recommend all you kids go and check him out.

The Buns All Surprises

IT WAS A COLD DAY LAST SATURDAY. COLD ENOUGH TO TURN THE ears red and make the nose run with the wet, smooth snot. And I sniffled.

But the day was outside, and we were inside. The basement of the SMU student center. The freshmen girls were there. They were all dressed in their bluejeans and their white turtlenecks. So was I. They wore perfume. I did not. We all sat in the plastic chairs in the room that looked like a hotel ballroom, waiting. Four hundred freshmen girls and I.

They wore the turtlenecks because that day they would get their bids. After months of rushing the sororities and attending the parties with aid of neither wine nor beer, after all the introductions and polite conversations about nothing, that day they would learn which house would have them. Would they wear the label of the Tri Deltas or the Gamma Phis? The Thetas or the Kappas?

Then the running of the pigs would begin. The name is not a flattering one, but I did not invent it. The girls would run through the streets, screaming like pigs, to their new sorority houses. There they would be greeted with the hugs and the new Greek-lettered jerseys that they would wear over the white turtlenecks.

And I, in my own well-made turtleneck, would run with them. Fear is nothing to be ashamed of. A man needs fear to remind him he is still alive. But I was not afraid. I knew a Gamma Phi, a senior. Her name was Kelley. Kelley was a good woman. She would be expecting me at the house.

It was time. The woman at the podium told the roomful of girls: "Unless you're quiet, you don't get to open your bids." Yells came from the crowd. They let her know they would not be quiet. Not today.

I turned to the one seated next to me. "What are you hoping for?" I asked.

"Go Gamma!" she screamed. "Whoooh!"

"Whoooh!" I told her. "Gamma rules!"

I was unsure whether Gamma rules or Gammas rule, but she did not correct me.

The woman at the podium said, "One, two, three … go!"

The girls all stood and opened the bid envelopes. The room became a great confusion of hair and perfume and yelling. It was as if a bomb had exploded. There is no other way to describe it. Girls from the front row rushed to the exit doors, walking on chairs as they went, screaming. Everyone wanted out. One girl fell. She rose to her feet and did not seem injured.

We ran outside and into the streets. The police had cordoned off the streets, and crowds of fraternity men, Fijis and Lambda Chis, lined the route to sorority row, waiting for the girls. The men drank beer. They wore their fraternity colors. A few held Super Soaker water guns that they trained on the girls.

The cold and the excitement showed through the girls' turtlenecks. As I ran with them, panting, feeling the bitter wind in my face, some girls still screaming, some saving their breath, I saw the tight bluejeans and the buttocks. They were the fine, well-shaped buttocks of youth, not yet ruined by cheese fries and sedentary lives spent sitting at desks. And I also felt the excitement.

We came to the Gamma Phi house. The women of Gamma Phi stood together, waiting for the pledges, their sisters. They had set up speakers on the porch. Loud '80s party music echoed off the surrounding buildings.

Kelley found me and yelled, "Tim!"

"Kelley!"

She pushed her way toward me, through the crowd, smiling. Her cheeks were red. She pulled the teal Gamma Phi Beta jersey over my head. We hugged as we'd never hugged before, as if it were the first time we'd hugged, which it was.

I felt prouder than I had ever felt before or have since. Everything seemed new and fresh. I understood why I had gone through the painful rush parties — or why I *would have* if I were a girl and 18 again — and why I had chosen Gamma Phi over Tri Delt and why I should never drink while wearing my letters. I knew what it meant to belong. Anything seemed possible.

"Go Gamma!" I said to Kelley. "Whoooh!"

"I think teal is your color," she said.

"Yes," I said. "Isn't it pretty to think so?"

Three Squad Cars Surrounded Us

I'D LIKE TO SHARE WITH YOU A STORY THAT RAN A FEW MONTHS BACK in the *Daily Oklahoman*, Oklahoma City's newspaper. Under the headline "Three Arrested for Not Wearing Pants," the story read:

"Three out-of-towners were caught red-handed — sort of — after police found them running around downtown Oklahoma City without pants.

"The men were booked into the Oklahoma City Jail on complaints of indecent exposure. Police found the trio, who were wearing only shirts, sitting on a curb in front of the Medallion Hotel about 2 a.m. Sunday.

"A female driver reported the incident. Arrested were: Bob Smith*, 28, and Timothy Allen Rogers, 26, both of Dallas; and Mark Jones*, 26, of Ardmore. All have since been released from jail."

There is, in case you are wondering, only one Timothy Allen Rogers, age 26, who lives in Dallas. That would be me. All I can say is, if they didn't make the beer so weak up there in Oklahoma, I wouldn't have had to drink so much of it.

For whatever reason, I have a predilection for getting naked in public. (I do it a lot in private, too, but that's hardly worth mentioning.) My parents were hippies. That might have something to do with it. When I was about 5 years old, my mom took me to a nudist camp. I innocently brought along my most prized possession: a new pair of binoculars. I'd been wearing them around my neck for about a week. A nudist-camp official demanded that I not only put away my binoculars but that I take off my clothes, which I had been hesitant to remove. Maybe that childhood trauma somehow caused my current condition.

And I don't just like to streak, which, by definition, means running. I also enjoy getting naked in public and just standing still. In my opinion, standing still requires much more courage. Although walking naked is pretty daring, too.

I once walked naked into a 7-Eleven with Roommate Joe, who was also naked, and ordered two Big Bites. We explained to the clerk that we were having a late-night snack attack. The one customer in the store at the time thought the whole deal was hysterical, but the clerk was dumfounded. He kept saying, "You cannot do this, you cannot do this," and we kept saying, "All we want is two Big Bites, and we'll be on our way," until he got on the horn to call for backup, and we thought it wise to leave.

Then there was the time when, having just received my diploma from the hallowed University of Notre Dame, I joined some friends for a celebratory naked midnight tour of the campus. We posed for pictures in front of various points of interest: naked with the statue of Jesus, naked on the steps of the administration building, naked in the fountain. It was a real hoot.

A few weeks later, though, one of the friends mailed the pictures to My Fair Lady, who was then living at home, and my future mother-in-law stumbled across them. She views nakedness as the unavoidable state that occurs between changes of clothes, and she thinks it should be kept as brief and private as possible. I had to write her a letter apologizing for being naked with Jesus (who, for the record, could plainly be seen smiling in the photograph).

Anyway, the good citizens of Oklahoma City apparently see things the way my mother-in-law does. I would have been happy to write an apology to the female driver who saw us running semi-naked toward the Medallion Hotel that night, but she ruined any chance of that when she picked up her car phone and called the police. Minutes later, as we sat on the hotel's curb waiting for My Fair Lady, whom we had put in charge of our pants several blocks earlier, three squad cars surrounded us.

Here's something fun to try: Next time you're in the hoosegow and a big Indian with a tattoo of a flame-spouting buffalo on his bare chest asks what you're in for, look him tenderly in the eyes and tell him, "Indecent exposure."

So last weekend, I returned to the scene of the streak for my court date. With a little bargaining, the city attorney agreed to a $500 fine and no jail time. That brought the cost of my adventure — including court costs, bail, and legal representation — to about $1,120. Considering the size of my offense, I'd say I was penalized rather stiffly. As I told the judge, though, I'm sure I've learned my lesson. Honest.

*Names have been changed because my colleagues have real jobs that they wish to keep.

114

I Prefer That Whoever's Driving Keep Both Eyes on the Road and the Other Massive Vehicles Traveling at High Speeds Thereon

AWHILE BACK, I GOT A JOB THAT REQUIRES A NASTY COMMUTE. Forty-five minutes, sometimes an hour, in each direction. But, as good fortune would have it, a dear friend of mine — I'll call him Beric — also works for the same outfit. So I figured: Right on. I'm all about the ride share.

But now, some three months later, it has all gone horribly awry. Our daily routine has turned Beric and me into … well, I guess you could call us a *couple*.

It goes like this: I arise at 6 a.m., taking care not to disturb My Fair Lady's slumber. If it is Beric's turn to drive, I sit on the couch, in the dark, and watch *SportsCenter* until he shows up. Beric is always late, I think because he can't leave his house without forgetting his purse.

I crawl, sleepy-eyed, into the car, and we proceed to the gym. I give Beric the silent treatment the whole way there to punish him for his tardiness. He gives me the silent treatment back, as is SOP.

We work out until 7:30. Beric further irritates me by complaining nonstop about his "fat ass" and "Beric thighs" and about how, since he weighs more than I do, he can't execute as many dips on the triceps apparatus as I can. He describes, in detail, what he ate the night before and how, contrary to what I might think, it conforms to his new diet. I irritate Beric by being naturally thin.

Then we shower. Let's just say that quickly lost its charm.

After the gym, Beric and I make a pit stop at an area coffee shop. There we bicker about whose turn it is to pay. If it's my turn, I point out that Beric always gets a coffee *and* a muffin, whereas I generally forgo the muffin, so really I should pay more like every third time and not every other. Oh, and did I mention we have matching stainless-steel coffee thermoses?

Next comes the commute proper, unless Beric needs to get gas, which he always seems to when we're running late — which, if he's driving, we always are.

During the trip, when I'm riding shotgun, I enjoy reading Beric's *Wall Street Journal*. Beric, though, he likes to chat. And he likes to look at me when he chats, to make eye contact, I suppose. This makes me nervous, because I prefer that whoever's driving keep both eyes on the road and the other massive vehicles traveling at high speeds thereon. I'll be reading the *Journal*, trying to ignore Beric's palavering, and I'll catch him out of the corner of my eye, looking at me, when I'm clearly not on the road and even more clearly pose no danger to us. So I'm compelled to interrupt my reading and look up — but not at Beric. If he's not watching the road, then someone has to, and with only two of us in the car, you figure it out. Consequently, Beric grows even more irritated with me for not looking at him when he's talking to me, and I get little reading done.

If I'm driving, Beric does charming things like announce, "This isn't going to be pretty," and expectorate laboratory-quality phlegm into the Money & Investing section of the *Journal*. I never read the Money & Investing section, but I still find this habit distasteful.

Having each consumed an entire thermosful of coffee prior to our arrival, Beric and I will not infrequently wind up at work in the bathroom together, in adjacent stalls, having concurrent bowel movements. So that's nice.

We lunch together. Not sure why. Old habits hard to break. More dietary concerns expressed. Postprandial bickering over the bill. Et cetera.

Then comes the drive home. The other thing I neglected to mention about Beric's driving is that, besides being unsafe, it's directionless. Always he picks the slowest lane. If, for instance, a light is on the fritz and traffic is backed up, Beric *loves* to invent alternate routes. Like Magellan this guy is. Always looking for the short cut. I offer directions from the passenger's seat. I'll say, "Aarfgk!" Or, "Echt! Wrong!" Or, "What the hell? No-no-no-no! Can't you see this way sucks even more?" He never listens.

On weekends, we watch entire football games together without speaking.

Do they have old, gay Jewish couples? Is there such a thing? If there is, that's us. We don't have sex anymore. We don't really even like each other. But we give meaning to each other's lives. Like an incurable disease that you fight at first but then learn to accept and come to terms with, so that it defines who you are. Beric and Tim, the leprosy couple.

I considered breaking up with Beric, my fat-keistered friend. But then I thought about all the gas. Not to mention the wear and tear.

Dwight Agnor Is a Professional Who Does Not Play Games

I AM A POWERFULLY BEAUTIFUL MAN. WHEN I VENTURE OUT ONTO THE boulevard, grandmothers are filled with a desire they haven't known since their own viviparous fields were fertile. Prepubescent schoolgirls feel a stirring they won't fathom for years to come. Nuns weep openly. Hard-core lesbians think twice. Bitches go into heat weeks ahead of schedule.

All the attention can get to be a bit much. But we all have our crosses to bear, and mine is built of broad shoulders, sinewy thighs, steadfast buttocks, and a manful visage seemingly chiseled from granite. I have sought solace all these years behind the printed page, where, unfettered by my shockingly good looks, I have been able to express my true self, my inner beauty, with a blend of wit, wisdom, and fart jokes.

But last week, I decided to abandon the life of letters and cash in on my hot bod. A radio commercial for the Manhattan Model Search made me rethink my choice of career. The MMS was in town to hold a series of open calls for prospective models, one of which would take place at the Grapevine Convention Center. A golden-throated MMS pitchman said, "You've seen us on numerous television talk-show and news programs and read about us in dozens of renowned publications, including the *New York Times*."

I thought, "I haven't read about you in any renowned publications, including the *New York Times*. But, you know, I bet models make a lot more money than writers, and I bet they enjoy more complimentary drugs and casual sex, too."

So it came to pass that I found myself, on a Friday night, filing into a room at the lovely Grapevine Convention Center with about 600 other aspiring models. A bald man, sort of a No Ad-brand version of Telly Savalas, ran the show, barking at us to move quickly and take our seats. As we did, everyone eyed each other, curious to see who else in Grapevine thought he or she was model-caliber attractive. I overheard one girl say to her friend, "She looks like a total slut," which appeared to me like a pot-and-kettle situation, because the girl who said it was wearing so much blue eye shadow that she herself looked like a raccoon that had lost a bar fight.

My own personal assessment of my modelability vis-à-vis the

Grapeviners' was: Bring on the cat tranquilizers and anonymous handjobs!

It turned out that No Ad Telly was actually Dwight Agnor, president of MMS. Once we were settled, Dwight Agnor introduced himself and then subjected us to a short video that further extolled the "unique and singular credentials" of MMS. Did you know that MMS is based in Manhattan and boasts 15 full-time employees? It's true.

The video ended, and Dwight Agnor barked more instructions. Stand up, three rows at a time, and file past him. Smile. Dwight Agnor needed to see if we had teeth, he said. Remove our eyeglasses and any heavy outer clothing, such as jackets. Those of us whom Dwight Agnor judged might win a placement with a modeling agency would be handed a brief form to fill out and asked to stay for a workshop later that night. The rest would be thanked for coming and asked to leave.

"Don't be insulted by how fast I work," Dwight Agnor said. "If you're not asked to stay, please don't ask me what's wrong with you. You're not ugly — most of you. I'm a professional. I'm not playing games."

I was sitting at the back of the room and got to watch him for about 15 minutes before my turn came. He did work quickly, that Dwight Agnor. Like a professional. A professional who was not playing games. As the Grapeviners walked past, he decided their fate without a moment's hesitation. To a lucky few he handed the slips of paper and the opportunity to live and work. Most, though, he sent to the ovens.

When he called for my row to stand, I arose with confidence. Perhaps I would find work as a catalog model. Perhaps the runway. Either way, I would never again spend a long night hunkered over a keyboard, clacking away to earn a writer's paltry wage. Oh, I might engage in some late-night hunkering, but only of the sort in which dangling modifiers are encouraged.

I approached Dwight Agnor, allowing his eyes the pleasure of my Adonic beauty. He, standing, backpedaled as we met, as if he were loathe to let the joyous vision pass.

"Smile," he said. I obliged. "Thank you for coming," he said. "You can go."

And that is how you narrowly avoided losing your columnist to the world of modeling. From the looks of things, you'll have him awhile longer.

My Forearms Burned From
Holding the Mattress

SOMETIME BACK, I ENTERED DWIGHT AGNOR'S MANHATTAN MODEL Search and got summarily rejected. Outwardly, I made as if I were unfazed. "Isn't it funny that Dwight Agnor found me too plain to be a model? Ha, ha." Inside, though, a little piece of me died. Part of my pancreas, I think.

But after a late-night binging on cookie dough and fried pork skins (and retching over the toilet to maintain my flat tummy), I said, "To heck with Dwight Agnor. I have cheekbones to die for and lashes that go on forever! I'll make it as a model even if I have to pose naked for an art class."

The next day, I rang the Art Institute of Dallas, which proved fruitless. A rather haughty young man told me I needed experience. "You can't just get up there and take your clothes off," he said. "Modeling is hard work. It requires holding a pose for three hours."

I wanted to tell him, "You'll rue the day you didn't hire Tim Rogers! You and Dwight Agnor. Maybe not tomorrow. Maybe not the day after. But someday soon and for the rest of your life. You'll flip through a *GQ*, and there I'll be, in a Tommy Hilfiger ad, gamboling on a beach in wet briefs." But the first rule in modeling is, you never burn bridges.

The folks at SMU, fortunately, weren't as selective, and I landed a gig as a nude model for Professor Barnaby Fitzgerald's painting class. On the appointed day, I arrived on time but, due to forces entirely within my control, critically hung over. I sized up the dozen or so students and determined that there were only two to whom I really wished to show my penis.

In walked Barnaby Fitzgerald, attired in a blue smock and Coke-bottle glasses. He took one look at the striking interplay of color between my ocher-green shirt and pallid face and decreed that the class would paint me standing in the shirt, propped against a pink Sealy Citation Ultra Plush single-size mattress that he dragged to the front of the room.

"And take off your pants," he said.

"The boxers, too?" I said.

"Just your pants," he said.

I dropped my pants. The class made appreciative-sounding oohs and aahs at my blue plaid boxers. Look at the colors, they said. Observe the patterns. See how his face is now turning a shade of avocado.

I struck my pose, leaning with my back to the Sealy Citation Ultra Plush, arms outstretched, gripping the sides of the mattress. And the students painted. And I stood. The smell of oil paints and turpentine filled the room. And I stood. Barnaby Fitzgerald wandered among the easels, admonishing his students not to abuse white, which is a color, he said, just like yellow. And I stood.

My forearms burned from holding the mattress. My back ached. My legs went numb from the knees down. At one point, my vision narrowed into a gray tunnel, my mouth drained of its saliva, and I could feel myself slipping out of consciousness. But I struggled to squeeze the blood back into my head. And manfully I still stood.

Then Jim showed up. Jim was himself a model and, wily veteran that he was, carried with him a canvas bag filled with all sorts of modeling paraphernalia, including a battery-powered clock. I had been advised to take breaks every 30 minutes, but I was unable to see the clock directly above my head and had no way of knowing when those 30 minutes had elapsed. Rather than risk ridicule for poor performance, I had been posing for upwards of 45 minutes. Like a timepiece-bearing St. Bernard for models in distress, Jim came to my rescue.

So Jim hung around and worked the timer and watched me model. On another break, Jim reached into his bag of tricks and produced naked pictures of his model friends, none of whom, let's just say, would have made the cut with Dwight Agnor's Manhattan Model Search. Jim also shared some "insider jokes" about nude modeling and hard-ons. So that was nice.

And then, when my modeling shift at long last came to an end, just when I thought I might collapse on the floor and cry, Jim invited me back to his studio where he could give me some "pointers." I'm sure it was just me, and Jim's intentions were nothing but noble, but going back to his studio for "pointers" sounded ... oh, like maybe it was a line out of a gay porno.

In any case, I felt fortunate to have survived my first outing as a model and didn't intend to pose a second time. I politely declined Jim's offer, put on my pants, and made haste out of there. That night, my modeling career thus ended, I kept the pork skins down.

"Ohh, oh!"

WHILE UP LATE ONE NIGHT LAST WEEK, AGAIN CONTEMPLATING suicide, I saw a commercial on the television that troubled me. It featured a montage of images depicting the recreational opportunities available downtown. A Stars hockey game, Dick's Last Resort, et cetera. It ended with a narrator saying, "Downtown Dallas: Are you up for it?"

I later learned, via journalism-style reporting, that the commercial was a joint production of the Central Dallas Association and the Downtown Improvement District, the relationship between which a CDA official described thusly: "We're like an octopus, and the DID is one of our tentacles."

What troubled me about the commercial was the question it posed. You want to answer, "Hell, yes, I'm up for downtown Dallas!" But hold on there. You might *think* you're up for downtown, but until you've actually made the trip, how can you possibly assess whether you've got what it takes to handle whatever downtown has in store?

I can tell you this: Japan thought it was up for a war against the U.S. of A. Magic Johnson thought he was up for a talk show. But Japan and Magic were both mistaken.

No. The only question about your ability to cope with downtown's offerings that you can answer with assuredness is *"Were* you up for it?" And since octopuses lack spines, meaning the DCA and the DID won't ask the right question, I went downtown and did.

I ventured first to Pioneer Plaza, where I met Stenio Rodriguez, a Brazilian tourist. Despite that country's wretched economy, Stenio and his three friends brought to bear on the plaza's bronze cattle an impressive array of consumer electronics. I introduced myself and asked if I could interview Stenio. He agreed.

"The story I'm writing is about a new ad campaign that the city of Dallas has on television," I told him. "The ad campaign asks, 'Downtown Dallas: Are you up for it?' This is an English phrase. Are you familiar with it?"

Stenio said, "Yah."

"Okay. So the question is: Were you up for it?"

There followed much discussion in Portuguese between Stenio and his colleagues. I gathered they were searching for a Portuguese translation of the question. I gathered they weren't finding one.

"Are you big, or something?" Stenio said. "What's the meaning?"

"Are you up for it, in other words, means, there's a lot to do. Were you prepared to handle it all?"

"Okay. So the question is?"

"So the question is, Were you up for it?"

"Ohh, oh!" Stenio said. More confabulating in Portuguese ensued. I said, "The question is, Have you enjoyed everything you've seen?" To which they all answered: "Oh, yes!"

I next approached a man sitting on a retaining wall near City Hall. He was wearing a black baseball cap and an extremely puffy black winter coat. Whether or not he had been up for downtown Dallas I'll never know, because he was not up for an interview.

I found James sitting against the east wall of McDonald's. He asked me if I had any change to spare. I told him I'd give him 50 cents if he'd answer a question. I told James, who preferred not to divulge his last name, about the commercial.

"So the question is," I said, "Were you up for it?"

"Naw," James said.

"Why is that?"

"Just probably because I'm stranded a little bit," he said. "You know, probably just being depressed."

I caught Charles Pierce coming out of the West End Lounge at 1 p.m. It was apparently much brighter and sunnier outside than inside the West End Lounge, because Charles had to squint hard and shade his eyes with his hand. I gave him the lowdown on the commercial and said, "My question to you is, Were you up for it?"

"I'm all for downtown Dallas," Charles said. "And I think the West End has been a little boost to help Dallas. And I hope that people will come down and utilize the facilities that have been put in."

Charles knew how to dodge a question. I pressed him: "But were *you* up for it? Personally?"

"Well, yeah," he said. "I don't do anything I'm not up for."

"At any point in the day, since you've been downtown, have you been worried that maybe you weren't quite up for it?"

"Well, it depends on what part of downtown you're talking about. If you're talking about from the transfer station to down south, they've done a good job, as far as I'm concerned. If you want to look over there at those beautiful trees that they planted — and they're blossoming — I think that's good for downtown Dallas."

As for me, after having visited downtown Dallas, I almost felt up for Plano. Or maybe even Ennis.

When I Stood, My Asscheeks Were in a Constant State of Floss

AS I TYPE THESE WORDS, I AM WEARING A PAIR OF PLAID FLANNEL boxers that I bought at the Gap. They're brown, size large, with one of those wide, well-built waistbands that your quality boxers have.

I mention this because, for the two previous days, I wore some panties that belong to my wife, and they weren't nearly as comfortable. And it wasn't due to inferior construction, either. One of the pairs came from Victoria's Secret. I understand they make top-notch panties.

It's like this: People seem pretty upset by this whole Marv Albert thing. Everyone's going, "That beaver-pelt hairpiece was gross enough, but now he's running around in women's panties, biting people? He's totally icky."

When I was 4 years old, I used to bite my friend Richie, and Richie was a hemophiliac, so I learned in a real first-hand, emergency-room way why biting is wrong. But I don't see how a guy's wearing panties could hurt anyone. If I put on some silk skivvies and maybe even a garter belt, no one's going to require a tourniquet and high-speed conveyance to the hospital for an injection of good old Desmopressin.

So before I joined the Marv fray, I did some research. My wife doesn't own any garter belts, but, as long as I didn't tell her, I figured she wouldn't mind if I borrowed her panties for a couple of days. On Monday morning, while My Fair Lady was taking a shower, I snuck into her walk-in closet and promoted panties from her dresser. I selected a powder-blue pair with the words "Victoria's Secret" stitched into the waistband, which had no actual panty material attached to it at the sides. I guess you'd call them bikinis. But they were pretty plain, with no frills. A good training pair, I figured.

I took the panties to the gym with me, where I planned to slip into them after my workout. That proved almost disastrous, because, honestly, you don't want the guys in the locker room to catch you putting on your wife's panties. So what I did was, after showering, I waited for the locker room to clear, and I quickly jumped into the panties. But then, trying to yank up my jeans before anyone walked in, I wound up hopping around in the powder-blue panties, which didn't have as much room in the crotch as I would have liked. I imagined knocking my head on one of the open locker doors and passing out on the floor, where the next guy in would find me lying, unconscious, in women's panties. But I made it out unscathed and unseen.

At first, I enjoyed wearing the panties. In front, they rode a little tight and down, and in back they rode a little narrow and up, but it was sort of fun. At the office, I found myself having conversations with co-workers, and all I could think was, "Right now, I'm wearing my wife's underwear." Just between me and Victoria, I had a dirty little secret.

By the end of the day, though, some serious support issues had arisen — as in, I was getting it in all the wrong places — and I was ready to take the things off. I snuck the panties into My Fair Lady's dirty laundry, taking care to put them at the bottom of the pile so she wouldn't notice.

Tuesday got ugly. I thought I'd upgrade to something a little more sexy, a little more feminine. I picked a pair of white briefs, this time of indeterminate make. They had lace trim in the front. When I put the panties on, they immediately crawled up my ass like a pack of wild dogs chasing a kielbasa. I won't even go into the frontal situation. Let's just say things were in disarray.

I spent the entire day at work adjusting myself, to no avail. Those underwear were mean, cruel, and they wouldn't give me a moment's respite. When I stood, my asscheeks were in a constant state of floss that I found way more bothersome than sexy. So forget about having a secret. The thrill was gone.

My research ended in a rather odd chain of events. That night, My Fair Lady and I had a few friends over to the house for dinner. When we were cleaning up, dealing with the wine and beer bottles, someone asked, "Do you guys recycle?"

MFL said, "The only thing Tim recycles is his underwear."

The unnamed friend then asked, "How's that program coming?"

At which point, MFL said, "Let's see," walked up behind me at the kitchen sink, grabbed my jeans, and pulled the waist back to have a look. After what can only be described as a pregnant pause, she exclaimed, "You're wearing my underwear!"

Needless to say, I had to do some quick explaining about my research.

Here, then, are my findings: If Marv Albert enjoys wearing women's panties, he sure as hell ain't wearing my wife's.

Burn! Burn! Feel the Burn!
Push It!

THIS IS A STORY ABOUT A MAN NAMED JOHNNY G AND HOW HE changed my life. As the legend is recounted in promotional materials, Johnny G is a rebel — a fitness rebel. "While others were busy embracing whatever fitness trend was fashionable," the materials read, "endurance cyclist Johnny G was embracing a set of sweat-soaked handlebars, turning his cranks over mountains, across deserts, and through horrendous weather. While others were frolicking on the apparatus du jour" — those carefree, exercising fools! — "he was pouring all of his strength, determination, and experience into a bike program unlike any other."

Johnny G created Spinning. And he saw that it was good.

Spinning, for those who don't know, is the "revolutionary stationary-bike fitness program." Not revolutionary as in "storm the Bastille and sharpen the guillotine," but revolutionary as in "an addictive blend of sweat, endorphins, and pure imagination." And pedaling in place. That is also part of the blend.

I will admit that I was skeptical when I first heard about Spinning and how it was taking the nation by storm. An aerobics class conducted on stationary bicycles? A roomful of people pedaling themselves nowhere but toward apoplexy?

But, as Johnny G says, "Spinning is the ultimate workout. It's non-impact, and, what's more, it's about mental development. Spinning teaches that making dreams come true requires effort."

I had an erotic dream the other night wherein Xena, the warrior princess, taught me some nifty moves with my broadsword. So I thought I'd see if Spinning could teach me how much effort is required to make that dream come true.

The first problem I had with the Monday Spinning class at my gym, the Fitness Furnace, was that it started at 6 a.m. Arriving on time meant getting up at 5:30. I don't know if anyone has told you this before, but it's still dark at 5:30. Really dark. I mean, it looks just like nighttime.

At the Fitness Furnace, I learned that Monday's class was for advanced Spinners. This did not embolden me. And the instructor, a disciple of Johnny G, must have sensed that I was a trouble-making pupil, because he put me at the front of the class, where I couldn't disrupt the Spinning process of my advanced classmates.

Before we got to work, the instructor turned off all the lights, except for the one that shone on the spinning disco ball. Then he lit some candles and put on soothing, ambient warmup music. The place took on sort of a mellow *MTV Unplugged* vibe. Speaking into a microphone while riding his bicycle, the instructor began the class by telling us, "Okay, close your eyes and pedal. Get the right and left sides of your brain to meet in the center. Circle, circle, circle. Pedal, circle."

I tried to meet my brain in its center, but I was distracted by the fear that I would shortly be asked to pedal in squares. After about 10 minutes of warmup, this fear was joined by dizziness, shortness of breath, and a persistent feeling that I was about to vomit.

My disposition did not improve when the instructor said, "All right, get ready to go up the mountain!" The music changed. A techno-trip-hop mix of a Jackson 5 tune assaulted the room: *Whomp-whomp-whomp*. "A, B, C. Easy as one, two, three." *Beep-beep-beep*. "Simple as do, re, mi."

The instructor barked into his microphone, "Spin, spin, spin! Come on, make it burn! Burn! Burn! Feel the burn! Up the mountain! Push it! Hey, you in the front, turn up the resistance on your bike!"

Shortly after we reached the top of the mountain, I decided to get off my Spinner for a drink of water and maybe to throw up. I forgot, though, that my feet were strapped to the pedals, and that the pedals on a Johnny G Schwinn Spinner are rigged like a tricycle's. As I tried to get off the bike, the pedals kept turning, with my feet still in them, nearly breaking both my ankles and throwing me into the candles. It was most definitely not an advanced maneuver.

When the class finally ended, an hour later — after we'd ridden over the Washington Bridge for a cool-down — I stumbled to the locker room. That's when my life changed. Sitting naked on a bench, trying to muster enough strength to stand in the shower, I remembered something Johnny G says: "To be alive is to be on the edge, to be in a place where you physically cannot handle what's happening."

It was then that I began to look forward to death.

To the Children of Africa, I can Only Say This: The Clothes Don't Make the Man

I WANT TO APOLOGIZE RIGHT HERE TO ALL YOU HYDROCEPHALIC, YET darling, African children I keep seeing on television who need my 36 cents per day to get something to eat. I'm afraid you kids are going to have to make do with whatever you can find in the back of the icebox, because last week I bought a $1,000 suit, and now I'm all tapped out. Actually, it cost $1,077 and some change. By my math, that comes to a little more than eight years of chow.

Terribly sorry.

It all began with a professional obligation that required a new dress shirt to fulfill. And maybe a coat. I'm in a line of work that usually requires nothing more than four hours of sleep and a mostly odor-free T-shirt, but for this one occasion, I figured I'd go first-class. Top notch. Whole hog. Let the high-school punks with their mothers' credit cards shop at Structure. George Zimmer can keep his guarantees and his Men's Wearhouse. No, a man of taste and distinction, a true gentleman, shops at Neiman Marcus.

So it came to pass that, accompanied by Squire Beric, my style consultant, I pushed my way through the glass doors and into the rarefied air of the downtown Neiman's. Neither Squire Beric nor I had ever been in the place, but it only took a brief debate at the store directory to determine that dress shirts were to be found in "The Man's Store" and not in "The Men's Room." That settled, we mounted the escalator.

"Ooh, chocolate!" declared a wide-eyed Squire Beric as we ascended to the second floor.

Below us, a lass was hand-dipping nut clusters into a vat of velvety Godiva brownness. I leaned over the escalator handrail to get a better look at those delicious treats — and conked the back of my head on the ceiling, nearly decapitating myself. This did produce no small amount of laughter from Squire Beric and disapproving stares from fellow shoppers.

Safely arrived in The Man's Store, feeling somehow more manful for just being there, I proceeded to communicate to the various sales associates my exact socioeconomic status by walking from one garment to the next, feeling its fabric, and remarking loudly to Squire Beric, "These pants are $595!" and, "Jesus shit!" and so on.

At length, with Sales Associate Michael's assistance, I found a blue shirt that only cost $75, or about what it would cost to feed a starving African for six months, which was somewhat less than I was prepared to spend. So I asked Michael to take me to his coats.

Michael was probably the most courteous and helpful sales associate I've ever had the pleasure of meeting. When I ventured that buying a suit, really, made more sense than buying a coat, on account of I rarely ever wear just a coat, Michael agreed wholeheartedly and showed me an exquisite, midnight blue Hickey-Freeman. And when I demonstrated the breadth of my fashion knowledge by feeling its lapel and asking if it was made of silk, Michael replied, without a soupçon of condescension, "No, sir. That's worsted wool." I had no idea what "worsted" meant, but I could tell by the way Michael said it that worsted was a good thing for wool to be.

The next thing I knew I was trying on the $1,000 Hickey-Freeman back in Michael's own personal fitting room, which featured not only your basic surround-a-mirror but also a nice view of Main Street and a couch for Squire Beric to rest his weary bones. And even though the slacks still needed to be cuffed, the Hickey-Freeman hung on my well-shaped shoulders like a dream. Standing before Michael's mirror, I was met with a vision of sartorial splendor.

No matter that it would take months to pay it off. No matter that my wife would kill me before she embarked on a retaliatory shopping spree of her own. No matter that African children would surely starve to death as a direct result of my profligacy. I wanted the Hickey-Freeman.

"I'll take it," I said, in a trance.

A small Spanish man appeared from nowhere and began tugging at my crotch and drawing on my ass with white chalk and mumbling in an impenetrable accent. I assume he was a tailor.

A footwear man brought in a natty pair of $185 Cole-Haan shoes so that the Spaniard might better measure the Hickey-Freeman's cuffs. The shoes felt so luxurious and I was so drunk on hyphens that I told Michael I'd take the Cole-Haans, too.

To the children of Africa and to my wife, I can only offer this: They say the clothes don't make the man. While it is usually the impoverished and ill-attired who say this and while I'm pretty sure it's bunk, take comfort in knowing that I am the same man I was before I bought the Hickey-Freeman (and the Cole-Haans). I love you all.

That, and you'll be happy to hear that I didn't buy the shirt.

Family Life

Now It's Just Me and the Girls

HERE'S A PARTIAL LIST OF WORDS I'VE USED, IN THE PAST, TO COMplete the sentence "I got ... ":

... drunk.

... lost.

... lucky.

... hornswaggled.

... giardiasis.

Another word recently joined that list, a word I never expected to utter in connection with myself. Last month, I got evicted.

I thought getting evicted was something that only happened to the sort of people who have head lice. And search though they have with giant tongue depressors, no nurse has ever found critters on my noggin. Despite this, I still received a certified letter instructing me in no uncertain terms to decamp.

Best I can figure, here's how it happened: While I was at work, behaving like a responsible member of the community and contributing to the Gross National Product, the roommate formerly known as Bathroom Boy (henceforth known as the Homewrecker) decided to hold a band practice in the house. This was bad, because the Homewrecker's band is not exactly what you'd call a chamber ensemble, and when we moved in, we signed a lengthy form that expressly forbade "creating a nuisance."

Myself, I'm a pretty tolerant fellow. I have a lenient definition of the word "nuisance." But one of our neighbors apparently had a stricter interpretation and called our landlord to let him know he didn't appreciate the Homewrecker's rock and roll and the volume at which he was playing it.

And that was that. Next thing I knew, the four of us (myself, Homewrecker, and our other roomies, henceforth known as Chrissie and Janet) were evicted — without even so much as a warning. No itchy scalp, no nothing.

To my ex-neighbor (and I have a pretty good idea which one made the call), I say this: Remember when we first moved in and came around to introduce ourselves and gave you our phone number in case there was ever a problem? And remember how you smiled and said you were sure there'd never be a problem, but if there was, then certainly you wouldn't hesitate to call? Well? Did you misplace the number?

I understand how that can happen, because in our haste to move out, we somehow misplaced 5 pounds of venison in the backyard, where I imagine it got nice and ripe after about three days in the heat. Sorry.

And to our supportive ex-landlord, I say this: We found a new house only two blocks away, and I know where I used to live.

Maybe the worst part about getting evicted is the Homewrecker no longer lives with us. We considered splitting up our foursome, with the two girls going their own way and the Homewrecker and I going ours, but the girls found a three-bedroom gig that was too convenient to pass up. So I said goodbye to the man I've lived with for more than a year. It was a sad parting, sort of like breaking up with a girlfriend. "I'm sorry. I don't want to live with you anymore." Then quickly, "But we can still be friends."

Now it's just me and the girls. My life has at last become the sitcom I always hoped it would. Plot line: Chrissy and Janet have to cook dinner for two men they are trying to impress, but everyone knows they can't cook, so I volunteer my culinary services. Larry accidentally steps in my soufflé and zaniness ensues. Mr. Roper makes an appearance in a polyester shirt and white belt.

You'd be surprised how a domicile's dynamics change when you go from a 1:1 male-female ratio to a 1:2 ratio. Whereas before I had some backup testosterone to balance things out, now I live in an estrogen-rich environment. When the living-room carpet "just doesn't work" because of mysterious compatibility conflicts with the coffee table and sofa, I have no one to validate my feeling that a rug "works" as long it lies flat on the floor. No, the rug gets moved.

All things considered, though, the new living arrangement agrees with me. Did I mention our place has a kidney-shaped pool? Amenities like that can quickly heal the scars of a traumatic eviction.

Just the other day, the Homewrecker dropped by for a swim. Since his new house lacks hot water and phone service due to roommate error, he has seen the nuisance of his ways, and since Chrissy and Janet are both kindhearted gals, he's welcome to share our concrete pond. As he luxuriated on one of our Kool Kat floating lounge chairs, basking in the sun and letting his rock-and-roll hair flow through the water's inviting blue sparkle, the Homewrecker wryly asked, "So guys, when are you gonna thank me?"

Laugh track.

Roll screen credits.

At $9.95, the Egg Slicer Was
Quite a Value

L ET ME FIRST EXPRESS MY HEARTFELT GRATITUDE TO WHOEVER CON-tributed the 4-quart Amco stainless-steel mixing bowl. It's a lovely mixing bowl. Some months or years from now, I will no doubt wind up getting drunk and running around the house wearing the Amco mixing bowl as a helmet. I have already determined that I have approximately a 4-quart head. So thank you for the wonderful helmet, too.

Which is not to say that I appreciate the mixing helmet any more than I appreciate the other gifts we received at our bridal shower. Groomal shower. Whatever you call it. My fiancée and I are progressive folk. We both attended the soiree. Last weekend, at my aunt's house, on a joyously sunny day, my fiancée and our friends ate little sandwiches and drank Santa Fe shooters or something — white wine, orange juice, cranberry juice, club soda — and we opened goodies from Crate & Barrel.

Every gift we received was perfect. The Amco mixing helmet, the Grand Bonanza barbecue tools, the Concept Housewares wok set — all perfect. We may have picked them all out, but you guys did a great job of actually buying them. Thank you for driving to the mall, finding the Crate & Barrel, securing the registry, and spending the money.

I'm serious.

Please don't come and take everything back. Especially the Kaiser Bakeware cookie sheet. That's one ass-kicking cookie sheet.

Okay. Maybe I'm feeling slightly ambivalent about the whole shower concept just now. But I'm not ungrateful. Really, I'm not. Here's the thing:

Why the hell's it called a shower? The term "shower" evokes images of a brief, life-giving rain that nourishes lush meadows and leaves the birdies and lady bugs feeling full of vim and vigor. From my limited experience, the sort of shower at which San Jose shooters and finger sandwiches are served involves much less rain and a lot more woks.

Showers are all about the acquisition of household accessories. For single people — for men, at least — thoughts of domestic utensils occupy about as much brain space as ideas about how to improve the molecular structure of polystyrene. But something happens at the onset of marital union. Heretofore unthought-of items gain a new prominence in daily conversation.

For instance, your fiancée will say to you: "Honey, we need this egg slicer."

This is what my fiancée said to me in the Crate & Barrel where we were carrying around a clipboard, registering for our shower.

"What the hell we need an egg slicer for?" I said. I assure you it sounded more tender than it appears in print. "I have survived for almost 26 years without an egg slicer. I'm fairly certain a sharp knife will cut clean through a hard-boiled egg."

"Honey, we need this egg slicer," she said.

So we registered for the Pedrini egg slicer. I would like to mention — again, not wishing to seem ungrateful — that none of you thoughtless bastards ponied up for the egg slicer, which was quite a value, I think, at $9.95.

That is what showers are for, the acquisition of woks and dinner plates and pepper mills and egg slicers. Without these essential items, your marriage is doomed to fail. You will wind up in divorce court claiming that your wife is an unfit mother and an alcoholic. Now that we've had our shower, and now that we own a set of eight Mogi Trading corn picks, our marriage will bring nothing but bliss. It will be the ultimate expression of God's love on earth.

However, if my wife should one day — God forbid — succumb to cancer or get run over by an Amtrak commuter train, I will first observe the appropriate period of mourning, but then I will remarry and do things differently.

Instead of having another shower, my new fiancée (who will merely be a pathetic emotional crutch and not a soulmate) and I will have a "procurement." We will eliminate the middleman. Our guests will be instructed to bring a check or money order made payable to Tim Rogers. No egg slicers. No salad spinners.

Everyone will eat burgers and Funyuns and drink St. Ides malt liquor. When the time comes to open gifts, our friends will gather around and watch as we open envelope after envelope filled with money.

"Oooh," guests will say together, as if the contents of each envelope were a complete surprise.

"Thank you," I'll say to whoever contributed the $30 money order. "Just what we need. Thirty bucks! How ever did you know?"

I Did Not Fantasize About Being Naked With Cokie Roberts

BACK IN THE SALAD DAYS WHEN I WAS A SINGLE LAD AND LIVING with Roommate Joe, back when the stock market was driven by good old valuation instead of liquidity and emotion, I had a dream. The dream involved Roommate Joe and me. The dream involved ... well, let's just say the dream involved certain acts that are illegal under the state of Texas' sodomy laws.

Oh, I'll come right out and say it: In the dream, I had a 12-inch tongue. Except my tongue wasn't a tongue, really. It was more like a penis. And I used it on Roommate Joe — who, oddly enough, was equipped with a woman's nether apparatus. (If this offends you, I apologize. But I'm just reporting the facts as they happened.)

When I awoke, I described my harrowing dream in all its horrific detail to Roommate Joe. If I remember correctly, he said something along the lines of, "Would that technically fall under the category of coitus or cunnilingus?"

Point being, Roommate Joe didn't go haywire and accuse me of harboring a homosexual attraction to him. As a man of science, he understood that neurologists have yet to unravel the mysteries of dream causation and that while Sigmund Freud assigned all sorts of meanings to various dream imagery, old Sigmund also smoked cigars and pipes like a madman until he got an ugly case of mouth cancer that required the surgical removal of a good portion of his face. So Roommate Joe thanked me for sharing my dreams with him and simply suggested that I stay out of the adult section at the video store for a while.

Then the salad days came to an end, and the main course arrived. I got married and moved in with my wife. (She thought that our living together would foster better communication.) And now, when I wake up, I never know what strife the night will have brought, because My Fair Lady is not a man of science.

I learned quickly that a married man should never dream about another woman. I don't care who that woman is or how minor her role in your dream. You will always get in trouble. Because if you dream about a woman, that means you were *thinking* about her. Some part of your small, disgusting, lecherous brain — maybe that part way in the back, near the part that remembers Sigmund Freud had mouth cancer — that part was thinking about another woman while you were lying in bed. With your wife.

I made the mistake of waking up one morning and sharing with My Fair Lady. "I had the strangest dream," I told her. "I had to give a speech in front of a large audience. And I didn't have any clothes on. And my teeth were falling out. And Cokie Roberts was sitting in the front row."

She said, "You fantasized about being naked with Cokie Roberts?"

"What? No. It was *horrifying*. I was frightened. Cokie Roberts is, like, 60 years old and looks like Nancy Reagan."

"Don't try to talk your way out of it. Pig."

And forget about having an innocuous, slightly homoerotic dream. Even a short one. Not a good idea.

I've found that the easiest way to stay out of trouble is to avoid dreaming altogether — just to be safe. About four fingers of over-the-counter cough syrup right before bed usually suppresses brain activity enough to do the trick. Of course, you can drink all the Robitussin you want, and it won't affect your wife's R.E.M. sleep. That's the other thing I learned: You can get in trouble for things you do in your wife's dreams.

At least once a month, we'll be getting ready for work in the morning, and I'll notice that My Fair Lady looks a little sullen. "What's wrong, baby?" I'll ask.

"You didn't save me," she'll say.

"Excuse me?" I'll say.

"I was swimming in the ocean and all these scary sharks were circling and they were about to eat me and I yelled, 'Tim! Help! Sharks are about to eat me!' And you were on the beach, playing badminton with that girl from *Baywatch*. What's her name?"

"You mean Yasmine Bleeth?"

"You fantasize about her, too? I meant Pamela Anderson. Pig."

I used to argue about these dreams. Now I know better. I just apologize and remind myself that things could be worse. At least My Fair Lady, unlike Roommate Joe, doesn't snore.

My Dad Whipped Me in a Street Fight

SHORTLY AFTER I WAS BORN, MY FATHER WAS IN A MESSY MOTORCYCLE accident. He is living proof that some things which don't kill you, instead of making you stronger, can just ruin your knee.

He has excellent elbows, though. This makes my father better suited for shooting pool and running up bar tabs than for other high-impact activities such as, say, wrestling. So that is what he taught me: how to shoot pool — and, to some extent, how to run up a bar tab, although my mentors in that field have been too many to blame my father solely for my accomplishments therein. My mom deserves some credit. But Dad taught me to shoot pool.

Most fathers and sons share an enthusiasm for one sport or another. Those who can't hunt, fish, shoot pool, or play some other bona-fide sport often take up golf. But the point is not the game itself. The point is that the father and son have a history with the game, that, whether they realize it or not, they see the game as something more than a mere contest. A single game's final score doesn't matter as much as the games and years that led up to it.

When I was 7 years old, my parents got divorced. My father moved out of the house, and I would go stay with him every other weekend. My favorite thing to do on our weekend visits was to shoot pool at a place called the Knox Street Pub. That is where he taught me.

He would give the bartender a few dollars, I'd grab the fistful of quarters, and we'd head to the Pub's back room, where the table was. He wore a leather cap pulled low over his eyes. On the jukebox, Louis Armstrong sang "Mack the Knife" and the Dave Brubeck Quartet played "Take Five," tunes that to this day take me to the Pub's back room when I hear them. We shot eight ball. Slop counted, because, due to my lack of height and ability, I sank more balls when I just shot hard and didn't aim. I drank Shirley Temples. My father drank Dos Equis.

My mother also took me to the Pub. It had been one of her favorite spots before the divorce, and she saw no reason to stop going in, even if it did mean sometimes running into her ex.

Now the Knox Street Pub is gone. A casual Chili's eatery replaced it years ago. But when my father and I see each other, we still shoot pool. I am taller and stronger than him now and, on a good night, a better pool player. He would disagree. But we always seem to find a joint that will allow two men to run up a $150 bar tab while they shoot pool and will then kick them out at closing time without calling them a cab.

Which is exactly what happened when my father recently came through town. With him busy being a neuroscientist and me just busy, we only see each other a few times a year. I guess we overcelebrated the occasion.

The next morning, I awoke with a fresh laceration on my right hand. Two deep, parallel gouges ended in a roughly lima-bean-sized chunk of missing flesh in the webbing between my thumb and index finger. It oozed and hurt like hell.

"Would you look at that," I said to my wife. "That hurts like hell."

"I hope it *does* hurt like hell," she said. "You deserve it for making me pick you two up at 3 in the morning. And when I got you home, I think you cooked an omelet."

I didn't recall cooking any omelets. But neither could I remember how I'd dissected my hand. The faintest ember of a recollection hinted that my father and I had wrestled in the road after getting kicked out of the pool hall. I figured that's how I'd cut myself, which hypothesis was supported by the grimy slacks that lay in a heap at the foot of the bed. Why we were wrestling, I had no idea.

I talked to my father a couple days after he'd left.

"How's your hand?" he asked.

"It doesn't seem to want to heal," I told him.

"You might want to get some antibiotic ointment. Human bites get infected easily."

"I remember now! You *bit* me."

I was taller and stronger than he was, and I might have even beaten him in pool that night (though he would again disagree), but, bum knee and all, my dad had whipped me in a street fight.

"Well," he said, "let that be a lesson to you."

Pour Some Sugar on Me

I T'S NOT THAT YOU LOOK FORWARD TO YOUR WIFE'S GOING OUT OF town. No, that's never the case. Your wife is your partner on this grand journey they call life. You are not whole without her. When she leaves town for a business trip, she takes a part of you with her, and there's no way you would look forward to that — even if the part she took with her were something small and not visible to other women, such as a toe.

Closer to the truth would be to say that you look forward to staying in town by yourself. The possibilities! No one to check in with about dinner plans — not that you mind checking in. The freedom! You can do drive-through at Taco Bell and eat six taco supremes on your way to catch that action flick, *Lethally Extreme Death Strike*, that your wife won't see with you. *Laissez les bon temps rouler!* You can, if only for one night, remember what it was like to be unencumbered by connubial responsibilities, car payments, and bad knees. Take a mental holiday to rejuvenate your troubled psyche. Align your chakras and attune your soul to the universe. Or you can drink heavily.

Chances are actually pretty good that you'll wind up exercising that last option, because when your wife goes out of town, one of your single-guy friends at work will inevitably find out and say, "Well, well, well. That makes you a bachelor for the evening, doesn't it? A stag in the woods. A loose cannon on the battlefield of love. The renegade who has it made won't be retrieved for a bounty. Let's drink!"

When your friend starts quoting Styx lyrics, you know you're in trouble. But you make an attempt anyway: "No, not tonight. I'm going to take it easy, maybe catch an early flick, then go home and align my chakras."

That's when your single-guy friend makes the sound, the sound every married man knows and fears: "Whu-pisch!"

"Stop it."

"Whu-pisch! Whu-pisch! Her whip is so long, she can hit you with it all the way from out of town! Whu-pisch!"

Married men fear the whip sound because there is no equal and opposite sound with which we can defend ourselves. Single men suffer the misfortune of not having a loving companion who will pop the pimples on their backs, but there's no sound for that. So, after work, you go have a drink at a bar near the office with your friend. But just one.

The problem with that plan, as your wife would happily point out if she were in town, is that there is no such thing as just one drink. Maybe in some fairy-tale land where kittens talk and the rivers run with sweet milk chocolate, but not here, not in the real world, where unscrupulous bartenders over-serve you, then demand that you hand over your car keys. In that world, there are four beers, two gin and tonics, and a Knob Creek bourbon on the rocks — with exactly two ice cubes.

"Did someone say kittens?" your friend says. "We could walk to the Pussyfoot Club."

"No, no. I'm not going to any topless joint. Cartender, ball me a taxi."

"Whu-pisch! Whu-pisch!"

On the main stage at the Pussyfoot, a woman uglier than Janet Reno goes through the motions to Def Leppard's "Pour Some Sugar on Me."

"Huh," you say to your friend. "I didn't know Janet had a tattoo of a spider web on her navel. Here, give her a dollar."

After you run out of money at the Pussyfoot, at around 1 in the morning, you stumble back to the first bar and have the bartender remove your office key from your key chain. Since your wife can't come pick you up and since you're an unencumbered stag on a mental holiday, you head to your office to download dirty pictures from the Internet. This is living! At the Australian Adult Sex Shop Web site, you find something called the Multispeed Seaman's Bride, which is priced at a very reasonable $47.95. You download pictures of it and e-mail them to a friend of yours as a joke, with the message header "I love you." Then you get yourself a Yellow Pages to use as a pillow and pass out on the office floor.

You wake up as your co-workers arrive the next morning. You pull yourself up to your desk and see you've got e-mail. It's from the business associate to whom you accidentally sent the picture of the Multispeed Seaman's Bride because his name sits right above your friend's in your address book. The business associate wants to know if you really love him.

And then you remember why you got married.

When We Landed, I Wasn't Sure Who Was in Worse Shape

THE THING ABOUT MY GRANDMOTHER NEEN IS SHE HAS ALZHEIMER'S. She is 80 years old and she has white hair and she oftentimes cannot recognize her children. Also, Neen has been known to build herself a blueberry-yogurt-and-turkey sandwich.

I don't want to sound indelicate. I love Neen dearly. Before the Alzheimer's, when I was child, we'd explore tide pools at her summer house in Portland, Maine. She taught me how to torture hermit crabs by turning them upside down so they have to crawl out of their adoptive shells to right themselves. All I'm saying is, I can't imagine blueberry yogurt and turkey joining forces to become a taste sensation.

"Hey, your turkey is in my blueberry yogurt!"

"Your blueberry yogurt is all over my turkey!"

"Mmm!"

I just don't see it.

The thing about me is, if you'll excuse the expression, I'm not real crazy about flying. Like I usually require at least four stiff, pre-flight medicinal cocktails to board an airplane without getting the fantods, and even with an additional two or three follow-up in-flight cocktails, I still basically go fetal when we hit turbulence. I know my fear is irrational. I've got some control issues. But bottom line: I find it unpleasant to sit strapped into an overly small seat in a metal tube that's kept aloft, 5 miles above the extremely impact-resistant earth, by the same principles on which a Frisbee operates.

So last weekend, when I escorted Neen from her summer home back to Dallas, we did not have a smooth flight. And I mean that in every sense. First of all, Neen didn't want to return to Dallas, which who could blame her? Portland is beautiful this time of year. Highs in the 80s, overnight lows dipping into the 50s. Soft-shell lobster $3.79 per pound.

Second of all, we hit turbulence practically before we pulled away from the gate. By the time we reached cruising altitude, my butt ached. Since my role was ostensibly to help Neen remain airworthy, I declined my usual preflight medicine, and my primary coping mechanism for in-flight fantods — besides sweating so aggressively from my palms that any reading material I might be trying unsuccessfully to read turns soggy — is to clench up as if I were attempting to grab my seat-bottom cushion with my asscheeks. You do this for about 20 minutes, believe me, and your butt aches. Buns of Steel has nothing on the in-flight fantods, in terms of firming up the old fanny.

And Neen — who, thank God, convinced herself in the early going that she was en route to Portland, probably as a coping mechanism of her own — she would make the observation that we were certainly flying through some rough air, weren't we? She would ask why the emergency exits were located so far aft, apparently spotting some sort of safety design flaw. Then she'd go through the whole thing again. You know, rinse and repeat: rough air, emergency exits; rough air, emergency exits.

I was ripping the seat cushion apart with my gluteals, palms sweating like a madman, and my grandmother wanted to talk about probably the two last things I needed at the forefront of my mind. There was like this mental wrestling match between Neen and me, she wanting to discuss meteorological conditions and emergency-exit-distribution theory and I wanting to discuss anything but.

I tried to distract Neen by asking her about the summer home in Maine, which worked fine until the captain, from the flight deck, had to tell us how many miles to Dallas and what temperature it was in Dallas, which was where we were headed, to Dallas. I began to think he had Alzheimer's, too. Every 15 minutes, it seemed, he reminded us that we were Dallas-bound. That would upset Neen's notion of a northeasterly flight vector, with Portland as our final destination, and so I would have to tell her the captain was probably confused and not to worry.

And all the while, I kept thinking that something way beyond my control would cause us to plummet to the earth, me unmedicated and so with sweat literally gurgling as it poured from my palms, where NTSB investigators would later comb the crash site and discover my charred remains with 24A's seat cushion lodged up my ass.

When we landed, I wasn't sure who was in worse shape — me, my grandmother, or the guy who sat to our right and had to suffer our two dysfunctions for three and half hours. I dropped off Neen at her "assisted living" apartment complex. She thought she had finally arrived at her summer house, on the water, in Portland. I hugged her, and she felt small, sort of like an upright vacuum cleaner. Then I drove away, behind the wheel and completely in control, living my own illusion.

The Secret to a Happy Marriage

P EOPLE OFTEN ASK ME, "TIM, WHAT'S THE SECRET TO HAVING A happy marriage?" People also ask me, "What were you thinking when you [insert ill-advised, buffoonish maneuver that endangered myself and possibly others and that has resulted in arrest and finger-printing and that will almost certainly require expensive legal proceedings to determine the appropriate restitutive punishment for]?"

I don't know the answer to the second question — which doesn't matter, because I have learned over the years that the second question is generally a rhetorical one. So either you can ignore it and just stand there and hang your head, staring at your shoelaceless sneakers and the black ink all over your fingers, or you can answer, "I wasn't thinking, Sir."

But I know the answer to the first question. And because I feel that we were all put here on this earth to help our fellow man, I will tell you the secret to having a happy marriage. And because research has proven that people retain information better when it is imparted anecdotally, I will tell you a story.

The other night, I was kicking it at Adair's. If you've never been to Adair's, imagine a really upscale, tastefully decorated bistro that serves its own brand of handcrafted ale and that has a guy in the bathroom who makes sure you don't shake more than is absolutely necessary. Then imagine the exact opposite. Adair's is a honky-tonk hole with a questionable ventilation system and an even more questionable clientele, is what I'm trying to say. Fabulous place.

So Adair's is pretty crowded, and I'm still kicking it, tossing back a couple loud-mouth sodas with the boys and girls from work on account of someone is "moving on to bigger and better things," when the bartender drawls over the PA, in what to me sounds like a real accusatory tone, "Tim Rogers, you have a call. Tim Rogers, you have a call at the bar."

Well, the co-workers have a sick sense for this sort of thing and can tell right away that the call must be from hymeneal headquarters, so they launch into a chorus of whip noises. As I walk toward the bar, everyone in the place turns to watch because at the table I just left, there are 15 people cracking imaginary whips like they're in the chariot race scene in *Ben Hur*, going, "Whu-pisch! Whu-pisch!"

A few opt to make pussycat noises. The bartender instructs me to pick up the call on the pay phone on the wall next to the bar, which pay phone is within ear- and eyeshot of my co-workers, some of whom are now standing on chairs so they can whip me from across the room.

Over the basic bar din and Hank Williams Jr. from the jukebox and plus now with the "whu-pisch"es and the "meow"s — I can see actual veins popping out of my co-workers' foreheads, they are straining to whu-pisch and meow so loudly — I can hardly hear My Fair Lady on the other end. I sort of have to hunker down and use my body as a sound shield and poke that little cartilaginous thing into the canal of my free ear.

"What's that in the background?" My Fair Lady asks.

"I'm being whipped," I tell her. "And also meowed. What's the problem?"

"It's 9 o'clock."

"I know you did not call me at a bar, requiring the bartender to summon me over the PA, just to tell me it's 9 o'clock."

"You said you were going to be at Adair's until 8. And it's 9 o'clock."

"Look," I say. "I was just about to leave. I'm going to have one more drink, and then I'm leaving."

She says there's no such thing as "one more drink," and we have to go over that whole thing again. I hang up and return to the "whu-pisch"es and "meow"s. When my co-workers ask who it was on the phone, as if they don't already know, I report that my wife called to tell me what time it was. More taunting ensues. My style is further jocked. Advice is freely dispensed, the upshot of which is that I should stay at Adair's and redouble my drinking efforts and go home late and loaded to teach My Fair Lady not to call me at a bar. They explain that if I go home now, My Fair Lady will have "hand," as in "the upper."

Despite the temptation, though, I do the right thing. I down a shot of So Co and head home, sober and not too terribly late. I show my betrothed that our marriage means more to me than boozing it up with co-workers.

Which brings me to the secret. Listen up. Lean in close. The secret to having a happy marriage is this: Never, under any circumstance, tell your wife where you're going to drink.

Wouldn't You Like to Be My Neighbor?

MY FAIR LADY AND I RETURNED HOME ONE EVENING LAST WEEK to find a red plastic plate sitting on our doorstep. To the plate were glued a plastic knife, a plastic spoon, and, opposite the knife and spoon, a fork and napkin. In the center of the plate, again affixed with glue, was a synthetic morsel of indeterminate composition. At first I thought the thing was a threat left by an artsy-craftsy stalker, the Party Store manifestation of his twisted, malevolent Dixie-brand fantasies.

But then My Fair Lady pointed out that the plate was a harmless invitation to a neighborhood meet-and-greet. Inside, under the light, I could see she was right. The particulars were written in black marker. It asked that we respond, if we pleased, but before I could request a family meeting to discuss whether we wished to attend, she had already made the phone call and indicated in the affirmative.

It wasn't that I didn't want to meet our neighbors. We've lived in our 'hood almost a year, so it was about time I met them. But the invitation said the party would commence at 7:30 and continue until "?". It was the "?" part that worried me, because I've had previous neighbors whom I've met, and, in my experience, there are only two possible situations that can result from meeting the neighbors: Either your neighbor tells you about how he belongs to the Judean People's Front and how every other weekend he does survival training in the woods for the apocalypse and eats grubs, and you think, "Oh, God, I live next to a possibly dangerous grub-eating freak"; or your neighbor tells you about his tomato plant, which tomato plant produced exactly 14 tomatoes this year (three more than last year), but last year's were sweeter, and you think, "Oh, God, I live next to a possibly dangerous tomato-eating freak." Either way, you don't want to hang out with them from 7:30 to "?".

But so anyway, My Fair Lady and I went to the party. It was two doors down, so we walked. I felt very European, doing all that walking. Assuming 20 seconds, tops, transit time, I figure we arrived at about 8:15. Fashionably late. We found 15 or so neighbors on the backyard patio, which was outfitted with citronella candles, an icy tub of assorted beers, and a table laden with tasty snacks, including a scrumptious phyllo-wrapped, baked brie (courtesy of Neighbor

Leigh, I later learned). After introductions were made, I quickly came to realize that several neighbors were definitely not using 16-ounce gloves to hit the sauce. These neighbors were strictly bare-knucklers, and the sauce looked to be in the early rounds an utter rout.

As I joined in the fight, and as genuine neighborly interaction got under way in earnest, I also realized that my neighbors were an all-right bunch. Better than all-right, even. Instead of standing around the backyard, boring each other with petty gossip about neighbors who either didn't show up or weren't invited, we … well, I guess we did stand around and gossip. But it was juicy gossip.

Like there's this one guy in the neighborhood who booby-traps the side of his yard with nails so that his neighbor won't drive over the grass when he's pulling in and out of the driveway. And this same Lawn Nazi has ladies show up at his house, late at night, in taxi cabs, which, come on, can only mean one thing, right? I had no idea this stuff was going on.

Before I knew it, about 10 of us had moved inside and it was 2 in the morning and we were telling dirty jokes. Someone said, "We ran out of liquor," and I said, "I've got a full bottle of Jim Beam at the house," and I stumbled out to fetch it. Actually, come to think of it, I'm not sure we ran out. I might have just said, "I've got a full bottle of Jim Beam at the house," and gone to get it.

After that, at around 4, Neighbor Brett and I manfully disassembled Neighbor Julie's toilet to see why it wouldn't stop running. Then we went next door to look at Neighbor Tammy's toilet so we could figure out how to put Julie's back together. Then My Fair Lady dragged me home, and I put a pizza in the oven and went to sleep (I am told the smoke alarms were very loud).

So now I have discovered the rare, third possible situation that can result from meeting your neighbors: binge-drinking followed by experimental plumbing followed by pizzacide. Chances are, if you take the risk and attend your neighborhood party, you won't get as lucky as I did. But think about it this way: If you don't show, the neighbors will talk about you behind your back.

In No Time, I Had Horny Ray Whole Again

I F YOU HAVE NEVER TRANSPORTED THE HEAD OF AN 11-POINT ELK, THEN you will, as I did, underestimate what it takes to get the job done properly. I promise you. Because unless you have experience in dealing with elk — like if you're an elkherd or a taxidermist — you have no idea how massive the head of an 11-point elk is, exactly. A four-door Saturn SL2, for example, does not have enough cargo room.

I came to this realization while trying to thwart my wife. Seven months gravid and bursting at the seams, My Fair Lady glows with a beauty seldom seen in this earthly realm. It's true. But the pregnancy has turned her into a fiendish decorator. Experts call it "nesting." I call it "moving all my stuff around so I can't find it" or, "If you don't quit it, I'll be forced to take drastic measures."

She started with the couch. One day, My Fair Lady determined that it didn't belong against the living-room wall. It had occupied that spot since the day we moved in and seemed to work just fine. We sat on it, enjoying many hours of television viewing. An untold number of guests sat on it, each one without complaint. Yet I came home one day to find it relocated to the center of the room.

Always open to change, I remarked, "What the hell? This is dumb."

She said, "Observe the way in which the couch, once merely a piece of furniture, now serves as a divider, creating an anteroom *here* and a more intimate living space *there*," or words to that effect.

My Fair Lady moved on to my personal area. Her gestational hormones raging wild, she rearranged my closet to make it more "efficient." I have been wearing the same outfit now for about a week because this increased efficiency has made it impossible to find any clean clothes. Then she wallpapered our guest room with a pajama-clad-teddy-bears print. Most unsettling, she took to calling it the "baby's room."

I had to do something. A man's house is, after all, his castle. If I didn't act quickly, my castle would become a … a big woman's place.

Nothing to me says "let down the portcullis" like an impressive piece of wall-mounted taxidermy. A little research led me to the head of the aforementioned elk. A once-hip y'all-ternative country bar in the midst of transitioning to a defunct once-hip y'all-ternative country bar was looking to unload some of its decor. I would have preferred a carnivore, perhaps a Bengal tiger, but whatever.

Five hundred dollars might seem like a lot to pay for an elk head. And it is. But the way I figured it, if you go the less-expensive route, you'll just have to pay for an upgrade three months down the road. I negotiated an installment plan.

Like I said, an 11-point elk has a big head. More to the point, it has a huge "rack," in outdoorsman parlance. Luckily the thing had taken a tragic spill not long ago, and, with one antler loose and the still-attached one sticking through a window, the head fit — just barely — in my back seat. On the way home, I named the elk head Horny Ray.

Back at the castle, I discovered that not only did the king have no horses, but his Super Glue could not put Horny Ray back together again. I scored some industrial-strength bonding agents from Ace Hardware. In no time, I had Horny Ray whole again — except, of course, for his body and legs. Sorry, Ray.

I'll skip the details of Horny Ray's installment because My Fair Lady still doesn't know about the sizable hole I left in a wall after my first attempt to mount him failed. But he wound up, after much struggling with rack-and-doorway spatial-relations problems, in my "office," where I "work."

Did I mention that Horny Ray was huge? To keep his antlers from hitting the ceiling, I had to mount him about 4 feet from the floor. This had the effect of putting his eyes at, well, eye level. And because my "office" is so small, one practically had to limbo under Horny Ray's nose to traverse the room.

My Fair Lady arrived home from work last Friday and admired my handiwork, sized up Horny Ray. Then she said "no" about 15 times, very quickly, each "no" louder than the preceding one. "That deer is *not* staying in my house," she said.

"He's not a deer," I said. "He's an elk. His name is Ray."

"I don't care. It's a big, ugly animal with horns. And it's dead. It probably has mites. You've brought mites into my house."

"You mean your nest. Horny Ray, you're not ugly."

As with most matters of domestic policy, My Fair Lady had the last word. Honestly, Ray did smell a bit musty. After he'd been hanging on the wall for an hour or so, my nose clogged up and began to whistle, which was unacceptable, because you can't very well conduct business with a whistling nose. And mouth-breathing is not an alternative.

So back to the bar Horny Ray went. It was an emotional good-bye. The only thing that might possibly fill the hole in my heart is a pinball machine. And a kegerator.

Problemo in the Baño

ALL THIS TIME, I'VE BEEN HEARING FOLKS COMPLAIN ABOUT THE Man, about how The Man is keeping them down and about how a brother can't get work on account of The Man et cetera. And all along, I've been thinking, The Man sure doesn't sound like a very nice person. Who does he think he is, anyway? The Man ought to be ashamed of himself.

Then, last week, I came to a terrible realization: I am The Man. Me. Yours truly. The Man. Or, rather, El Hombre.

It shook out like this: My Fair Lady had been making noise about hiring a maid for months. You know, someone to drop by every other week or so and tidy up, pay a little attention to that area behind the toilet that hasn't been cleaned, so far as I know, ever. As My Fair Lady pointed out, we are busy professionals. After a hard day of sending e-mail at work, we're not going to come home and have the energy or inclination to dust. As for the weekends, well, in addition to being busy professionals, we're also active young people. Outdoor recreational activities and social engagements take priority over soap scum. And television, too. We have to watch our programs.

I was against the hiring of a maid for socioyuppienomic reasons. Because, let's face it, "maid" is just a more palatable term for "servant," and I didn't want to be the sort of person who has a servant.

"Greetings, peasant. I am Tim, lord of the manor. Clean well behind the toilet, or I shall raze your hut."

Plus I was pretty sure this servant would require payment. Well, but My Fair Lady would not be denied. A friend of ours had a maid who had a sister who was available on an every-other-Monday basis. Lupita, I was told, came from a small village in Mexico and did not speak English. But she was eager to clean. So that was good. A poor Mexican woman. A villager, no less. And monolingual. How elegantly stereotypical. I was looking forward to watching her clean my house so that I could really hate myself.

Lupita arrived at 7:30 sharp in the a.m. with a small child in tow. I thought that was a nice touch. A club foot or harelip or something would have been effective, but it appeared healthy — outwardly, at least — and I only experienced a moderate-to-heavy level of self-loathing as I ate my cereal flakes and watched *SportsCenter*. The small child sat quietly and watched baseball highlights. Lupita attacked the place with a mop.

When I returned home after "work," the refreshing scent of lemon-flavored bleach greeted me. Not a dust bunny in sight. Kitchen looked like a commercial set. Sparkling floor. Spotless stove. I sat down with a beer, turned on the tube, and thought, Maybe I can get over this guilt. I mean, Lupita needs work, so really we're helping her. She'll clean our house for a couple of years, save money for school, learn HTML — and English — and one day have her own Web page. It's the least we can do.

Then I got up to go to the bathroom and saw that all was not right with the lord's manor. Apparently Lupita had been a little too liberal in her use of bleach and had cleaned most of the porcelain right off the bathtub. And then I noticed that she had washed the white towels with the blue bath mat, thereby turning the former a hue called, I think, dusty Amish lapis lazuli. And she had spilled some bleach on the hallway hardwoods. And, unexplainably, a blade from the bedroom ceiling fan lay on the floor, broken off at the metal arm.

I wanted to hang her, but My Fair Lady, through an interpreter, learned that Lupita was very sorry for the "problemo in the baño." She claimed no knowledge of the broken ceiling fan. Naturally, she couldn't pay for the damage, so we busted her down from $50 to $40 per visit and gave her a second chance.

All of which I was relating to a friend — how frustrated I was with my maid for turning our towels blue and messing up our tub and denying responsibility for critically wounding our ceiling fan — when it hit me: I am whining about the help. My maid. A poor woman whom I have deprived of the $10 every other week that she probably sends home to her family in a Mexican village. Now they won't be able to afford that new straw roof for their hut, and they'll get wet whenever it rains. All because the rich gringo was too lazy to clean his own house. In short, I realized that I am The Man. Next thing I know, I'll be playing golf.

These Three Fish, We Were Told,
Would Get Along Famously

ON OUR MANTELSHELF SITS AN ALLEGEDLY FRESHWATER AQUARIUM. I believe it holds 2 gallons. It is definitely hexagonal. A visitor to the house not long ago, a fish lover apparently, took notice of the aquarium and drew near to inspect it.

"Where are the fish?" he asked.

Whereupon I fell to my knees and began sobbing uncontrollably. "Where *are* the fish?" I wailed. "Oh, our dear fish! Our poor, dear fish."

Because the thing is, we don't have any fish. Not anymore. They've been dead, oh, I'd say almost two months now. You know how when *60 Minutes* does a segment about the kids who can't go outside to play during daylight hours, ever, because they have xeroderma pigmentosum, and exposure to sunlight would basically cause their eyes to explode? And you know how when Lesley Stahl interviews the parents of the little girl who was accidentally killed when the parents took her picture but forgot to turn off the flash? And you know how when the parents take Lesley on a tour of the little girl's bedroom, and her bed, her dollhouse, her closet — everything — looks *exactly* as it did the day the Fuji did her in, because the parents can't bring themselves to clean the place out and turn it into something useful, such as an office? Well, that's the way My Fair Lady and I are with the aquarium. We don't have the strength to drain it.

We got the aquarium as a Christmas present. The kindhearted lass who gave it to us said, "I know giving pets as gifts isn't usually recommended, but these tanks are totally low-maintenance. They're idiot-proof!"

So My Fair Lady and I paid a visit to PetsMart. We spent half an hour picking out fish. The Fish Woman counseled us on matters of fish temperament and underwater placement of plastic flora. She sent us home with two guppies in one plastic baggie and a black molly in another. These three fish, we were told, would get along famously.

Black Molly was the undisputed aggressor. She chased her aquarium mates in circles, nipping at their tails. Frick and Frack took to hiding among the plastic plants, venturing out only for food. But they were no match for Black Molly, and within a week, Frick's once proud tail was in tatters. Or it might have been Frack. We had trouble telling them apart. Whichever fish it was, Black Molly pursued him or her tirelessly, until either Frick or Frack was left with so little tail that he or she could hardly swim. One morning, we found him or her not swimming with the fishes, just lying on the nontoxic, epoxy-coated black decorator stones at the bottom of the tank.

Frack's — or Frick's — days were numbered. My Fair Lady and I awoke each morning expecting to find another casualty. We spent our evenings in the living room, watching the aquarium, bathed by the soothing hum of its 3-watt air pump, discussing whatever fish behavior we had observed during the day. We caught ourselves at dinner parties boring other couples with stories about how Black Molly hogged two food flakes and wouldn't let Frack — or Frick — eat just one, even when we tried to distract Black Molly by tapping on the tank and dropping a flake on the other side for Frack. Or Frick, if that happened to be the surviving fish. It was embarrassing.

One day I caught My Fair Lady standing at the aquarium with a 10-inch bamboo skewer, the sort used for shish-kebabbing.

"What do you think you're doing?" I asked.

"I'm punishing Black Molly," she said.

MFL demonstrated her technique. Whenever Black Molly made a move for Frack's — or, again, it could have been Frick's — tail, MFL would "spank" Black Molly with the skewer. Unconvinced by my argument that mollies did not respond to negative reinforcement as well as, say, dolphins, MFL continued her program for several weeks, until, despite her efforts, Frack — could have been Frick — died.

Then Black Molly died. Frick and Frack both got flushed, but I sealed Black Molly into a dry Hefty OneZip gallon-size storage bag and took her to PetsMart, hoping to learn what had killed her. But when the Fish Woman put the plastic bag on a table, Black Molly began flopping around like … well, like a fish in a Hefty OneZip storage bag.

"She's not dead yet!" I screamed. "I put her in the bag before she was dead. Quick, water!"

The Fish Woman put Black Molly into a cup of water and watched her swim for a second. She (the Fish Woman) explained that Black Molly was as good as dead — and not because I'd put her (Black Molly) into the Hefty. The Fish Woman indicated a white substance befouling Black Molly's scales. She said the technical term for it was "ick."

"What causes 'ick'?" I asked.

"You could have high nitrate levels in your tank," she said. "Or it could just be from stress."

I didn't mention the skewer. I just nodded and said, "Stress?" like it was an impossibility and our house was the most relaxing place on earth, for fish and mankind alike.

Babies Make Good Bait

SO I'VE GOT THIS KID. A BOY. HE'S TWO OR THREE WEEKS OLD. Somewhere in that neighborhood. I haven't enjoyed a surfeit of beauty sleep recently, and with my looks has gone my mind. It's hard for me to recall *precisely* how old this kid is. Is it important? Let's say he's well short of a year.

Not terribly useful around the house is one way I'd describe The Little Chit. Due to an underdeveloped musculoskeletal system and general hobbledehoyishness, he can hardly hold his head upright when I leave him unattended in the bathtub. Much less is he able to take out the trash or clean leaves out of the gutters, et cetera. So far, he's only proven himself adept at waiting for the naked window in diaper changings to piss indiscriminately on everything within 3 feet. Not that pissing indiscriminately on everything, especially if The Little Chit can increase his range, isn't a valuable skill. Just that it hasn't ameliorated *my* life much.

I hope that doesn't sound selfish.

Well but here's the thing about babies, the thing that I've been telling myself during the sleepless nights, the thing that has kept me from blowing out the pilot lights and turning up the gas. I heard that when it comes to attracting honeybuns, babies are the *ne plus ultra*. They work like scented Weedless Willy Worms with "corkscrew" action. Bass can smell those Willy Worms before they even hit the water. Can't resist them. Hardest part about fishing with Willy Worms is struggling to hold up your stringer at the end of the day as you pose for the pictures.

Leastways that's what my colleagues who've had babies tell me.

Imagine then my giddy anticipation when My Fair Lady and I recently took The Little Chit grocery shopping at the 24-hour Tom Thumb. Because just as bass lurk in the grassy, shady environs under sunken logs, so do SMU coeds and post-workout, Lycra-clad professional kippies stroll the well-lit, bounty-lined aisles of the 24-hour Tom Thumb. It is truly an angler's paradise.

For our outing, we arrived at approximately 6 o'clock on Thursday evening. Prime time. Kippies were visible in the parking lot, which is a lot like spotting bass hitting flies while motoring out to your secret hole on the lake. You're tempted to ease off the throttle and get to casting straightaway.

(Small aside here: I've only been bass fishing once in my life, so if it's not anything like that, forgive me. Please make up your own appropriate bass-fishing analogy and use that instead.)

In the lobby, I secured one of those shopping carts with an aft-mounted baby seat. First time I'd ever used one of those. It made the cart ride a little high in front, and, consequently, she tended to get a little loose on me in the turns. With some foodstuff in the bow, though, she handled fine.

I got my first strike at the deli counter. I was waiting to have my turkey sliced. The Little Chit was slumbering in his seat, looking "cute" and "small." Up walked a hungry-looking dame. In fishing parlance, she was a lunker, which is a good thing to be if you're a bass, a bad thing if you're a dame. But, as the saying goes, you've got to land the first fish before you can catch the second. She spotted The Little Chit, smiled. I tightened my drag, prepared to set the hook. Then the dame lost interest and walked away. Dumb bass!

There in the deli section, I shook my fists at the rafters and cursed the gods. "I laugh and hoot at ye!" cried I. "Ye've knocked me down, and I am up again. Come, Tim's compliments to ye. Come and see if ye can swerve me. Ye cannot swerve me, else ye swerve yourselves! The path to my fixed purpose is laid with iron rails, whereon my soul is grooved to run."

My fellow Tom Thumb shoppers, apparently, were not Melville fans. Dumb shoppers!

Anyway, I checked The Little Chit to see if he'd snagged some weeds, which can adversely affect his corkscrew action. Nothing. He was all systems go. Very frustrating.

And so it went for the remainder of our shopping trip. I got a couple strikes on the cereal aisle. Two kippies shopping in tandem showed some interest near the salty snacks. But by the time we reached the checkout line, while my cart was loaded, my stringer remained empty. Alas.

Once home, I mentioned to My Fair Lady how disappointed I was in The Little Chit's performance at the grocery store. "I trolled our son all over that store," I told her. "I didn't try the pet food aisle, true. But come on. How does a man go to the 24-hour Tom Thumb with a baby — an extremely young one — and not land a single honeybun? I think this tot might be defective."

She looked at me for minute. Then, like she was kicking me in my one good leg, she said, "A good craftsman never blames his tools."

enough